Python Automation Made Easy: A Beginner's Guide to Building Time-Saving Bots and Scripts

Peter M. James

Table of Contents

Table of Contents 3

Part I: Introduction to Python and Automation 6

Introduction 7

    Why Automate? 7

    Here's what automation can give you: 7

    How Python Makes Automation Easy 8

    Who This Book Is For 9

    How to Use This Book 9

    Final Thoughts Before We Begin 10

Chapter 1: Getting Started 11

    1.1 Installing Python and Setting Up Your Environment 11

    1.3 Writing and Running Your First Python Script 15

    1.4 Python Basics: Variables, Loops, Functions 18

    1.5 Understanding Modules and Packages 22

Part II: Core Automation Skills 26

Chapter 2: Automating Files and Folders 27

    2.1 Working with the OS: `os`, `shutil`, and `pathlib` 27

    2.2 Renaming and Moving Files in Bulk 31

    2.3 Organizing Folders Automatically 34

    2.4 Creating File Backups 38

    2.5 Project: File Organizer Bot 43

Chapter 3: Web Scraping and Automation 48

    3.1 Introduction to Requests and BeautifulSoup 48

    3.2 Extracting Data from Websites 52

    3.3 Handling Web Forms and Sessions 57

    3.4 Automating Browsers with Selenium 62

3.5 Project: Job Listing Scraper 67

Chapter 4: Automating Emails and Messaging............................. 73

4.1 Sending Emails with smtplib 73

4.2 Reading Emails with imaplib... 78

4.3 Using Email Templates and Attachments 82

4.4 Messaging with WhatsApp/Telegram APIs 86

4.5 Project: Automated Daily Email Reporter 90

Chapter 5: Working with Excel, CSV, and PDF 95

Why Automate These File Types? 95

5.1 Reading and Writing CSV Files.. 95

5.2 Automating Excel with openpyxl... 99

5.3 Generating Reports and Charts 103

5.4 Reading and Merging PDFs with PyPDF2 106

5.5 Project: Automated Expense Tracker................................... 110

Part III: Taking Automation Further 115

Chapter 6: Scheduling and Triggers... 116

Why Scheduling Matters.. 116

6.1 Using Python's `schedule` and `time` Modules 116

6.2 Setting Up Cron Jobs (Mac/Linux)..................................... 120

6.3 Using Windows Task Scheduler 124

6.4 Project: Daily System Cleanup Script (Sneak Peek) 128

Chapter 7: Desktop and GUI Automation................................... 134

7.1 Controlling the Keyboard and Mouse with `pyautogui` 134

7.2 Automating Tasks with Screenshots and Clicks 137

7.3 Simple Image Recognition for GUI Tasks 141

7.4 Project: Desktop App Login Bot.. 145

Part IV: Wrapping Up and Moving Forward 150

Chapter 8: Best Practices and Beyond 151

8.1 Debugging and Error Handling.. 151

8.2 Managing Secrets (Passwords, API Keys)......................... 155

8.3 Structuring Scripts for Reuse 160

8.4 Introduction to Version Control with Git 165

8.5 Next Steps in Your Automation Journey............................ 170

Appendices.. 174

A. Quick Python Syntax Reference 174

B. Common Python Automation Libraries 176

C. Useful Tools and Resources 177

D. Automation Project Ideas 178

Final Thoughts 179

Part 1: Introduction to Python and Automation

Introduction

Welcome to **Python Automation Made Easy** — a beginner's gateway to using Python to automate the repetitive stuff in life. Whether you're tired of renaming files manually, copying and pasting data from emails, or filling out the same online forms again and again, this book is for you.

Imagine having a little digital assistant — a bot — that does those dull, repetitive tasks for you. That's the power of automation, and by the end of this book, you'll be building those bots yourself.

Let's get started by answering the most obvious question first.

Why Automate?

Have you ever found yourself:

- Renaming dozens of files one by one?
- Copy-pasting the same text into emails every morning?
- Downloading reports, opening them, filtering data, and creating summaries — every single week?
- Checking websites multiple times a day for updates (prices, job listings, etc.)?

We tend to accept these chores as "part of the job" or "just something I have to do." But the truth is: **most repetitive digital tasks can be automated**, and you don't need to be a professional programmer to do it.

Here's what automation can give you:

- **Time**: Free up hours each week.
- **Accuracy**: Say goodbye to human errors.
- **Speed**: Let scripts do in seconds what takes you minutes.
- **Peace of mind**: Have scripts send you reports, reminders, or even messages while you sleep.

The first time I wrote a Python script to automatically rename a batch of 300 images from my phone, I felt like a wizard. It took 15 minutes to write and 3 seconds to run — something that would've taken me half an hour manually. That was the moment I knew automation was a superpower.

How Python Makes Automation Easy

There are many tools and languages you could use for automation, but Python is special — especially for beginners. Here's why:

1. Readable and Friendly

Python code reads like English. Look at this:

```
for file in files:
    print(file)
```

Even without knowing Python, you probably guessed: "This prints each file in a list." That's Python's charm — low barrier, high power.

2. Great Community and Libraries

Python has a massive community and a rich ecosystem of libraries. Need to:

- Scrape a website? Use `BeautifulSoup` or `requests`.
- Work with Excel? Try `openpyxl` or `pandas`.
- Automate the mouse and keyboard? Enter `pyautogui`.
- Send an email? `smtplib` has you covered.

Chances are, someone has already written a library to do what you need — you just have to learn how to use it.

3. Cross-platform and Free

Python works on Windows, Mac, and Linux. It's open-source and completely free. Once you learn it, you can run your scripts anywhere.

Who This Book Is For

This book is for you if:

- You're a complete **beginner** to Python or coding in general.
- You work with a computer daily and have a few tasks you'd love to **automate**.
- You've heard about automation but don't know **where to start**.
- You've written some Python before but never used it for **real-world tasks**.

You don't need a computer science background or a math degree. You just need **curiosity**, a laptop, and a bit of patience.

Whether you're a student trying to streamline study tasks, an office worker drowning in spreadsheets, or a hobbyist who loves tinkering with tech — you'll find practical, useful scripts here that you can use or customize.

How to Use This Book

We've structured this book as a **hands-on journey**. Each chapter builds on what came before, with practical examples and mini-projects to reinforce your learning.

Here's how to get the most out of it:

Code Along

Don't just read — *type the examples out*. Even if it feels repetitive, this is how you internalize syntax and logic.

Tinker with the Scripts

Every example is a starting point. Modify file names, change loops, add your own logic — this is how you make the scripts yours.

Try the Projects

Each chapter ends with a real-world mini-project. These are great ways to consolidate what you've learned and build something useful right away.

Revisit as Needed

Some chapters may feel dense at first. That's okay. Bookmark them and come back when you're ready. Automation is a skill — and like all skills, it grows with use.

Final Thoughts Before We Begin

Automation isn't just about saving time — it's about empowering yourself to do more with less effort. It's also fun, satisfying, and strangely addictive. Once you automate one annoying task, you'll start spotting automation opportunities *everywhere*.

Chapter 1: Getting Started

Before we start automating anything, let's make sure you're set up and ready to go. In this chapter, we'll walk through how to install Python, choose a beginner-friendly code editor, write your very first Python script, and explore just enough of the language to get you going with real automation tasks.

Certainly! Here's the expanded and refined **Section 1.1: Installing Python and Setting Up Your Environment**, written in a clear, concise, conversational tone, with in-depth commentary, expert tips, and hands-on implementation examples.

1.1 Installing Python and Setting Up Your Environment

If you're going to build automation scripts, your first step is getting the right tools in place. Think of this as setting up your workbench before you start crafting your first robot. In our case, that robot is Python — and once it's installed properly, you can begin automating almost anything on your computer.

Let's walk through everything you need to do to get Python installed, configured, and ready for action.

What Is Python?

Python is a programming language that's famously easy to read and learn. It's also incredibly powerful. It's used by everyone from Google engineers to high school students automating their homework folders.

And the best part? It's free, open-source, and works on any computer.

Checking If You Already Have Python Installed

Before installing Python, it's a good idea to check if it's already on your machine.

Open your terminal (Command Prompt on Windows, Terminal on macOS/Linux) and type:

```
python --version
```

or

```
python3 --version
```

If the response shows something like `Python 3.10.8`, you're all set and can skip to the next section. If you see an error or a version below 3.6, it's time to install or update Python.

Installing Python (Step-by-Step)

Step 1: Download Python

Go to the official website:
☞ https://www.python.org/downloads

You'll see a big yellow button for downloading Python. It usually recommends the latest version for your operating system (which is exactly what we want).

Step 2: Run the Installer

- **Windows Users:**
  Double-click the downloaded `.exe` file.
  Important: On the first screen, check the box that says **"Add Python to PATH."**
  This makes sure you can run Python from anywhere in your terminal.
  Then click "Install Now" and follow the prompts.
- **macOS Users:**
  Open the downloaded `.pkg` file and go through the installer steps.

macOS might also prompt you to install command line developer tools — go ahead and do that if prompted.

- **Linux Users:**
  Most modern distros already come with Python 3. If not, you can usually install it via the terminal:

```
sudo apt update
sudo apt install python3
```

Step 3: Confirm the Installation

Once the installation is complete, verify it by running:

```
python --version
```

or

```
python3 --version
```

Still not working? Try closing and reopening your terminal or restarting your computer. Sometimes the PATH update takes effect only after a restart.

Installing pip (If Not Already Installed)

pip is Python's package manager — it lets you install external libraries and tools that make automation possible (e.g., sending emails, clicking buttons, scraping websites).

In most cases, pip comes pre-installed with Python 3.4 and above.

To check:

```
pip --version
```

If pip isn't found, try:

```
python -m ensurepip --upgrade
```

Once installed, you can use it like this:

```
pip install requests
```

13

This installs the popular `requests` library, used for handling HTTP requests (handy for web automation).

Testing Your Setup with a Simple Script

Let's now write a very simple script to test if everything is working as expected.

Open any text editor (even Notepad will do for now) and paste this:

```
# hello.py
print("Automation test: Python is ready to go!")
```

Save it as `hello.py`.

Now, in your terminal, navigate to the folder where you saved the file, and run:

```
python hello.py
```

You should see:

```
Automation test: Python is ready to go!
```

Success! You've just run your first Python script.

What's Next After Installing Python?

Now that Python is installed and working, your next task is choosing a proper code editor — a place where you'll write and run your automation scripts. While you *can* write Python in Notepad, you'll want something smarter — like VS Code or Thonny — that gives you autocomplete, syntax highlighting, and a nicer experience overall.

We'll cover those in the next section.

Quick Recap

- We verified if Python was already installed.
- You learned how to install Python and `pip` from scratch.
- You tested your setup with a real Python script.

You're now officially a Python user.

From here, we'll explore how to set up your editor, write more complex scripts, and gradually start building your automation toolkit.

1.3 Writing and Running Your First Python Script

You've installed Python, chosen your editor (VSCode or Thonny), and you're staring at a blank screen. Now what?

This is where the real fun begins. Let's walk through writing and running your very first Python script—step by step—so you can get a feel for what automation looks like in action. We'll also break down what each line means, so you're not just copying code, but understanding it.

What Is a Python Script?

A script is just a plain text file with a `.py` extension that contains Python code. When you run it, Python executes the code line by line. Think of it as a recipe: each line is an instruction, and Python is your very obedient kitchen assistant.

Creating Your First Script

Let's start with something classic—but useful. Open your editor (VSCode or Thonny) and create a new file named `hello_automation.py`.

In that file, type the following:

```
# hello_automation.py

print("Hello, world of automation!")
```

That's it—your first script.

This single line uses the built-in `print()` function to output text to the screen. It's the programming equivalent of saying "Mic check."

If you're using Thonny, just press **F5** or click the **Run** button. If you're using VSCode, open the terminal (`Ctrl+`` or from the menu: View → Terminal), navigate to the folder where your file is saved, and run:

```
python hello_automation.py
```

You should see:

```
Hello, world of automation!
```

Congratulations—you just wrote and ran your first Python script.

A Slightly Smarter Script: Automate a Greeting

Let's build a script that's a little more dynamic. Say you want a personalized greeting.

Replace the code in `hello_automation.py` with this:

```
# greet_user.py

name = input("What is your name? ")
print(f"Welcome, {name}! Your automation journey starts now.")
```

Now run the script. It will ask you for your name, and respond with a custom message.

If you enter:

```
What is your name? Priya
```

It will output:

```
Welcome, Priya! Your automation journey starts now.
```

This introduces you to two core ideas:

- `input()` gets user input from the terminal.
- `f""` strings let you insert variables into text (this is called *f-string formatting* and it's incredibly useful for creating dynamic messages).

Working with Files: Your First Task Automation

Let's do something that feels a bit more like real automation: creating a file and writing some content into it. Here's a script that generates a text log automatically.

```
# create_log.py

from datetime import datetime

now = datetime.now()
timestamp = now.strftime("%Y-%m-%d %H:%M:%S")

with open("automation_log.txt", "a") as file:
    file.write(f"Script ran at: {timestamp}\n")

print("Log updated.")
```

What this script does:

- Gets the current time.
- Formats it in a readable way.
- Opens (or creates) a file called `automation_log.txt`.
- Appends the current timestamp to that file.

Every time you run this script, it logs the time it was executed. You've just built a simple, yet practical automation: **timestamped activity tracking**.

What You've Learned (and Why It Matters)

- **How to create a script**: You now know how to start a new `.py` file and run it in your editor.

- **How to print and take input**: These are essential tools in every automation—think user prompts, status messages, or configuration wizards.
- **How to work with files**: Much of automation involves reading or writing to files—logs, data exports, reports—so this is foundational.

Even with these basic tools, you can begin automating things like:

- Logging daily habits or tasks
- Collecting user feedback in a file
- Timestamping events on your system

Pro Tip: Start Small and Build Confidence

When I wrote my first automation script, I didn't build anything revolutionary. I automated the creation of weekly folders for a project. It was tiny—but the moment I saw it work, I was hooked. Start small. Celebrate the wins.

The goal at this stage isn't complexity—it's confidence.

1.4 Python Basics: Variables, Loops, Functions

Before we dive into building bots and automating your daily routines, it's important to understand the basic building blocks of Python. These are the tools you'll reach for again and again—whether you're automating file management, scraping websites, or scheduling reminders.

In this section, we'll walk through three essentials: **variables**, **loops**, and **functions**. They're not just "programming concepts"—they're the language your scripts will speak every day.

Variables: Storing Your Data

A variable is simply a name for a value. Think of it like a labeled container that holds something—text, numbers, or even more complex data like lists or dictionaries.

Here's a basic example:

```
name = "Zara"
age = 29
height = 1.68
```

You've now stored a name, an age, and a height. The = sign doesn't mean "equals" in Python. It means "assign the value on the right to the variable on the left."

You can use these variables like this:

```
print(f"{name} is {age} years old and {height} meters tall.")
```

Python automatically figures out the type of data—no need to declare it explicitly, which makes scripting faster and more intuitive.

Loops: Repeating Actions Efficiently

Automation is all about doing repetitive tasks without manually repeating yourself. That's where **loops** come in. They let you repeat an action multiple times, automatically.

The `for` loop

If you want to greet a list of people, you don't want to type `print()` for each one:

```
names = ["Zara", "Leo", "Mina"]

for person in names:
    print(f"Hello, {person}!")
```

This loop says: for every item in the `names` list, do this thing (in this case, print a greeting).

19

The `while` loop

This loop runs **as long as** a condition remains true:

```
count = 1

while count <= 3:
    print(f"This is message number {count}")
    count += 1
```

You'll use `for` loops more often when working with lists or files. `while` loops are more useful for waiting on conditions—like checking for a file to appear or retrying an action until it succeeds.

Functions: Reusing Code Like a Pro

A function is a named block of code that you can run whenever you need it—without rewriting it every time. If loops are about repeating actions **now**, functions are about repeating logic **later**, wherever and whenever you want.

Let's say you need to greet users in multiple scripts. Instead of copy-pasting your greeting code everywhere, you could write:

```
def greet(name):
    print(f"Welcome, {name}! Ready to automate?")
```

Now you can call this function with different names:

```
greet("Ava")
greet("Noah")
```

Functions also help you:

- Break big problems into smaller pieces
- Avoid repetition
- Make your code easier to test, read, and debug

You can also return values:

```
def square(number):
    return number * number
```

```
result = square(4)
print(result)   # Outputs: 16
```

This becomes especially powerful in automation when you want to:

- Process and return data from a website
- Generate dynamic filenames
- Evaluate success/failure of a task

Bringing It Together: A Simple Automation

Let's write a short script that uses all three concepts.

```
# reminder_bot.py

def remind(task, times):
    for i in range(times):
        print(f"Reminder {i+1}: {task}")

task = input("What do you want to be reminded about? ")
repeat = int(input("How many times should I remind you? "))

remind(task, repeat)
```

When you run this, it will ask you what task to remind you about and how often. Then it uses a **function** (remind), a **loop** (for i in range(times)), and **variables** (task, repeat) to print reminders.

Try it with:

```
What do you want to be reminded about? Take a break
How many times should I remind you? 3
```

You'll get:

```
Reminder 1: Take a break
Reminder 2: Take a break
Reminder 3: Take a break
```

This may seem simple, but this is automation—you're already replacing a repetitive task with a repeatable system.

Why This Matters

If Python were a language, then variables, loops, and functions are its grammar. Mastering them allows you to express any idea or solution clearly. They're the difference between someone dabbling in code and someone solving problems with it.

And in automation, clarity is power. Your goal is not just to write code that *works*, but to write scripts you (and others) can understand and reuse weeks or months from now.

1.5 Understanding Modules and Packages

As you start building more complex scripts, you'll quickly realize something important: you don't have to write everything from scratch. Python comes with an enormous library of prebuilt tools, and it lets you organize your own code into manageable pieces. This is where **modules** and **packages** come in.

Let's demystify these two concepts and explore how they can supercharge your automation projects.

What Is a Module?

A module is simply a Python file—a `.py` **file**—that contains reusable code: functions, variables, classes, or even entire programs. When you use a module, you're borrowing functionality someone else already built (or that you wrote earlier), so you can focus on your actual task instead of reinventing the wheel.

You've already used a module, even if you didn't realize it:

```
from datetime import datetime
```

Here, `datetime` is a module. It gives you tools to work with dates and times without manually building a calendar system. That's the power of modules: abstraction and convenience.

Here's another one:

```
import math

print(math.sqrt(25))
```

This imports Python's built-in `math` module and calls its `sqrt()` function to calculate the square root.

That's it. You've officially worked with modules.

Creating Your Own Module

Say you write a script that contains a handy utility function:

```
# helpers.py

def format_name(name):
    return name.strip().title()
```

Now, in a separate file, you can import and use it:

```
# app.py

from helpers import format_name

user = input("Enter your name: ")
print(f"Formatted: {format_name(user)}")
```

Just make sure `app.py` and `helpers.py` are in the same folder. This ability to split functionality into different files helps you keep code organized and maintainable—a lifesaver as your automation scripts grow.

What About Packages?

A **package** is a collection of modules grouped together. It's a directory (a folder) that contains an __init__.py file (even if it's empty), signaling to Python that this folder is a package.

Why use packages? Because they help you organize related modules under a single umbrella. Think of it like folders within folders. If you're automating tasks across different domains—email, files, web scraping—you might create a package like this:

```
automation_tools/
│
├── __init__.py
├── email_tools.py
├── file_tools.py
└── web_scraper.py
```

Now you can use:

```
from automation_tools.email_tools import send_email
```

And you're pulling functionality from an organized, modular structure.

Installing External Packages with `pip`

Beyond Python's built-in modules, there are **tens of thousands** of packages available on PyPI—the Python Package Index. These are third-party tools made by developers to save you time.

Let's say you want to work with Excel files. Instead of building an Excel reader from scratch, you can use `openpyxl`.

Open your terminal and install it with:

```
pip install openpyxl
```

Then use it in your script:

```
from openpyxl import Workbook

wb = Workbook()
sheet = wb.active
sheet['A1'] = 'Hello Excel'
wb.save('example.xlsx')
```

In a few lines, you're generating an Excel file—a task that would take significantly longer without this package.

This is how automation becomes powerful: by stacking simple tools in clever combinations.

Pro Tip: Don't Fear the Imports

New coders often hesitate when they see multiple `import` statements. Don't. Think of them as ingredients. If your script is a recipe, then `import` statements are just grabbing the right tools from the pantry.

Learning to find and use good packages is half the battle in automation. Python's ecosystem is mature and generous—there's a package for almost everything.

Wrapping Up

Modules and packages are more than technical features—they're what make Python scalable and collaborative. By learning to structure your code using these building blocks, you're laying the groundwork for more maintainable, readable, and reusable automation.

What's especially beautiful is how this lets you build **your own toolkit**—your personal automation library. As you create more scripts, you'll start reusing functions, grouping tools, and building packages tailored to your workflow.

Part II: Core Automation Skills

Chapter 2: Automating Files and Folders

Few tasks are as repetitive—and frankly, tedious—as managing files on your computer. Manually renaming dozens of files, organizing downloads into folders, or backing up important documents are all tasks ripe for automation.

In this chapter, you'll learn how to take control of your digital clutter using Python. We'll explore built-in libraries like `os`, `shutil`, and `pathlib`, and use them to rename, move, organize, and back up files. You'll even build your first real automation project: a File Organizer Bot.

2.1 Working with the OS: `os`, `shutil`, and `pathlib`

When you're trying to automate daily tasks with Python, a large part of what you'll do involves interacting with your computer's file system. That means reading directories, creating folders, moving or copying files, and checking if something exists before taking action. Thankfully, Python has robust tools built in for exactly this purpose.

The three main modules we'll use are:

- `os`: one of the oldest and most foundational modules for file system interaction.
- `shutil`: short for "shell utilities," this module focuses on file operations like copying and moving.
- `pathlib`: a modern, object-oriented module introduced in Python 3.4 that simplifies working with filesystem paths.

Each serves a unique purpose, and when used together, they can handle just about any file-based automation task you need.

Navigating Your File System with `os`

The `os` module gives you access to environment variables, system-level information, and basic file and directory handling. It's been part of Python from the beginning, and while it's slightly lower-level than `pathlib`, it's still widely used.

Here's how you can use it to list files in a folder:

```
import os

directory = "/path/to/folder"
for item in os.listdir(directory):
    print(item)
```

This will print out everything inside the given directory—both files and folders.

To check if a file exists or if something is a directory:

```
file_path = "/path/to/file.txt"

if os.path.exists(file_path):
    print("It exists!")

if os.path.isdir(file_path):
    print("It's a directory.")
```

Creating a folder is just as straightforward:

```
new_folder = "/path/to/new_folder"
os.makedirs(new_folder, exist_ok=True)
```

The `exist_ok=True` flag prevents errors if the folder already exists.

Moving and Copying with shutil

Where `os` ends, `shutil` begins. Need to move, copy, or delete a file or entire directory tree? `shutil` is your go-to module.

To copy a single file:

```
import shutil

shutil.copy("report.txt", "backup/report.txt")
```

This copies the file to the new location. If the destination directory doesn't exist, you'll get an error—so it's good practice to check or create it using `os` or `pathlib`.

To move a file:

```
shutil.move("old_folder/data.csv", "new_folder/data.csv")
```

This will move the file, overwriting the destination if a file with the same name already exists.

To remove a folder and everything inside it:

```
shutil.rmtree("old_backup")
```

Be cautious—this operation is **not reversible**.

Why `pathlib` Is a Game-Changer

If you're starting fresh, I recommend leaning into `pathlib`. It brings the power of object-oriented programming to file paths, making code easier to read and less error-prone.

Let's list all files in a directory using `pathlib`:

```
from pathlib import Path

folder = Path("/path/to/folder")

for file in folder.iterdir():
    print(file.name)
```

Need to filter by file extension?

```
for file in folder.glob("*.txt"):
    print(file.name)
```

Creating directories with `pathlib` feels more natural too:

```
backup_folder = folder / "backups"
backup_folder.mkdir(exist_ok=True)
```

Want to check if a file exists?

```
file_path = folder / "report.txt"

if file_path.exists():
    print("Found it!")
```

And renaming a file is as simple as:

```
file_path.rename(folder / "renamed_report.txt")
```

Using / to join paths instead of `os.path.join()` makes everything cleaner and easier to manage.

How These Tools Work Together

You don't have to choose just one. In practice, many developers use `pathlib` for path management and pair it with `shutil` for copying or moving files, while occasionally falling back on `os` for tasks like environment variables or low-level path manipulation.

Here's an example combining all three:

```
from pathlib import Path
import shutil
import os

source = Path("/Users/you/Documents")
backup_dir = source / "backup"

backup_dir.mkdir(exist_ok=True)

for file in source.glob("*.pdf"):
    shutil.copy(file, backup_dir / file.name)
```

This script backs up all `.pdf` files in the directory to a `backup` folder. Clean, simple, and effective.

Final Thoughts

Mastering file system automation opens up so many possibilities. You can organize your files by date, type, or project. You can automate backups or clean up messy directories. Python's trio of `os`, `shutil`, and `pathlib` make all of this accessible—even for beginners.

2.2 Renaming and Moving Files in Bulk

Renaming and relocating multiple files by hand is tedious and error-prone—especially when the files follow inconsistent naming patterns or are scattered across folders. This is where Python's automation capabilities truly shine. With just a few lines of code, you can clean up entire directories, batch rename files, and move them into organized subfolders.

This section will walk you through building simple but powerful scripts using the `os`, `shutil`, and `pathlib` modules. We'll cover common tasks like adding prefixes, changing file extensions, and relocating files based on criteria such as type or name pattern.

Understanding the Problem

Let's imagine you've downloaded 500 photos from your phone to your PC. Their names look something like this:

```
IMG_001.jpg
IMG_002.jpg
IMG_003.jpg
...
```

You want to rename them to something more descriptive, like:

```
Vacation_001.jpg
Vacation_002.jpg
```

At the same time, you'd like to move these into a dedicated folder—perhaps even grouped by file type or project.

Doing this manually could take hours. Let's automate it.

Renaming Files with `pathlib`

The `pathlib` module makes renaming files intuitive. Here's a script that renames all `.jpg` files by adding a custom prefix:

```
from pathlib import Path

folder = Path("/Users/you/Pictures")
prefix = "Vacation_"

for index, file in enumerate(folder.glob("*.jpg"), start=1):
    new_name = f"{prefix}{index:03}.jpg"
    file.rename(folder / new_name)
```

This example uses `enumerate()` to number the files and renames them with leading zeros (e.g., `001`, `002`), which helps keep them in order.

Changing File Extensions

Sometimes you'll encounter files with the wrong or missing extensions. You can fix them in bulk like this:

```
for file in folder.glob("*.jpeg"):
    new_name = file.with_suffix(".jpg")
    file.rename(new_name)
```

The `with_suffix()` method is handy for correcting or unifying file formats.

Moving Files into Subfolders

Let's say you want to separate all your `.jpg` and `.png` files into two folders. You can automate that easily:

```
import shutil

image_types = ['jpg', 'png']
```

```
for ext in image_types:
    subfolder = folder / ext.upper()
    subfolder.mkdir(exist_ok=True)

    for file in folder.glob(f"*.{ext}"):
        shutil.move(str(file), str(subfolder / file.name))
```

This script creates folders named JPG and PNG, then moves each image into
the appropriate folder based on its extension.

Conditional File Moving

Want to move only files that match a certain keyword? This comes in handy
for sorting documents or naming images based on event tags.

```
keyword = "invoice"

for file in folder.glob("*.pdf"):
    if keyword in file.name.lower():
        destination = folder / "Invoices"
        destination.mkdir(exist_ok=True)
        shutil.move(str(file), str(destination / file.name))
```

You now have a script that filters and moves files based on their names—a
huge timesaver for sorting reports, downloaded bank statements, or even
scanned receipts.

Organizing by Date

Using metadata to organize files can add structure to chaos. Here's how to
move files into subfolders by the year and month they were last modified:

```
import datetime

for file in folder.glob("*.*"):
    mod_time =
datetime.datetime.fromtimestamp(file.stat().st_mtime)
    year_month = f"{mod_time.year}-{mod_time.month:02}"

    dest_folder = folder / year_month
    dest_folder.mkdir(exist_ok=True)
```

```
shutil.move(str(file), str(dest_folder / file.name))
```

This script checks each file's last modified time and creates folders like
2023-07, 2023-08, etc., moving the files accordingly.

Final Thoughts

The ability to rename and move files in bulk is a powerful skill that
simplifies everything from digital photography to office workflows. With
Python, you're no longer limited by manual processes or clunky batch
scripts.

What's more, these scripts are easy to adjust and repurpose. Whether you're
sorting photos, cleaning a download folder, or preparing datasets, these
automation tools let you reclaim your time.

2.3 Organizing Folders Automatically

In today's digital age, it's easy to accumulate hundreds or thousands of files
scattered across your computer. Whether it's photos, documents, music, or
project files, managing these can quickly become overwhelming. The good
news? You don't have to manually organize them anymore. With Python,
you can automate the entire process, saving time and ensuring everything is
always neatly sorted.

In this section, we'll explore how you can automatically organize your files
into folders based on categories like file type, creation date, or even custom
naming conventions. This is especially useful for dealing with large
collections of files that need constant organization, such as downloads,
documents, or media files.

Setting Up Your Folder Organization

The first step in any automated organization process is deciding how you
want to categorize your files. There are several strategies you could use:

- **By File Type**: Organize files based on their extension (e.g., all .pdf files in one folder, all .jpg images in another).
- **By Date**: Group files by the year and month they were created or last modified.
- **By Project or Category**: For documents or media files, you might want to create a system that sorts based on the project name, department, or topic.

Let's walk through each of these strategies, starting with a simple script to organize files by their extension.

Organizing Files by File Type

If you have a folder full of mixed media—like images, text documents, and spreadsheets—you can automate the process of sorting these into subfolders based on file type.

Here's a Python script that does just that:

```python
from pathlib import Path
import shutil

# Define the folder to organize
folder = Path("/Users/you/Downloads")

# Create subfolders for different file types
file_types = {
    'Images': ['.jpg', '.jpeg', '.png', '.gif'],
    'Documents': ['.pdf', '.docx', '.txt'],
    'Spreadsheets': ['.xlsx', '.csv']
}

# Iterate over all files in the folder
for file in folder.glob("*.*"):
    for category, extensions in file_types.items():
        if file.suffix.lower() in extensions:
            # Create a subfolder for the category if it
doesn't exist
            category_folder = folder / category
            category_folder.mkdir(exist_ok=True)
            # Move the file into the appropriate subfolder
            shutil.move(str(file), category_folder /
file.name)
            break
```

In this script:

- We define a dictionary where each key is a folder name (e.g., 'Images', 'Documents'), and the corresponding value is a list of file extensions that belong to that category.
- The script then loops through all files in the `folder` and checks if their file extension matches any in the categories. If it does, the file is moved to the corresponding subfolder.

This approach ensures that all files are categorized neatly, making it easy to find files by type without manually sorting through everything.

Organizing Files by Date

If you prefer to organize your files based on when they were created or last modified, you can use the file's metadata to sort it into folders named by year and month.

Here's an example:

```python
from pathlib import Path
import shutil
import datetime

# Define the folder to organize
folder = Path("/Users/you/Documents")

# Iterate over all files in the folder
for file in folder.glob("*.*"):
    # Get the last modified time
    mod_time =
datetime.datetime.fromtimestamp(file.stat().st_mtime)
    year_month = f"{mod_time.year}-{mod_time.month:02}"

    # Create a subfolder based on the year and month
    date_folder = folder / year_month
    date_folder.mkdir(exist_ok=True)

    # Move the file into the date-based folder
    shutil.move(str(file), date_folder / file.name)
```

In this script:

- We use `file.stat().st_mtime` to get the last modified time of each file.
- The `datetime` module helps format the date into a string, creating a folder structure like `2023-04` or `2023-05`.
- The files are then moved into these folders, which ensures they're organized chronologically.

This approach is especially useful for automatically managing documents that get added over time, like invoices, reports, or photos.

Organizing Files by Custom Category

Sometimes you might want to organize files based on a custom category. For example, you might have files named after projects or clients, and you want to group them into project-specific folders. Here's a script that moves files based on a keyword in their names:

```
from pathlib import Path
import shutil

# Define the folder to organize
folder = Path("/Users/you/Projects")

# Define the categories based on keywords in filenames
categories = {
    'Project_A': ['proposal', 'draft'],
    'Project_B': ['report', 'final'],
}

# Iterate over all files in the folder
for file in folder.glob("*.*"):
    for category, keywords in categories.items():
        if any(keyword.lower() in file.name.lower() for
keyword in keywords):
            # Create the category folder if it doesn't exist
            category_folder = folder / category
            category_folder.mkdir(exist_ok=True)
            # Move the file into the category folder
            shutil.move(str(file), category_folder /
file.name)
            break
```

In this case:

- Files with specific keywords in their names (like "proposal" or "draft") will be moved into corresponding project folders such as `Project_A` or `Project_B`.
- You can adjust the `categories` dictionary to include your own project names and keywords.

This script helps maintain organized folders when you work with a variety of client or project-based files.

Final Thoughts

Organizing folders automatically with Python can save you hours of tedious manual sorting. Whether you're grouping files by type, date, or custom criteria, Python gives you the power to set up efficient, scalable systems for managing your data. And the best part? Once your automation scripts are set up, they'll continue to work seamlessly in the future.

2.4 Creating File Backups

One of the most important tasks we all face is protecting our data. Whether it's personal files, work documents, or critical business information, we know that data loss can be devastating. That's where creating backups comes in. In the digital world, it's not a matter of *if* something will go wrong, but *when*— and having a backup in place can save you from losing everything.

With Python, creating automatic backups becomes a simple, repeatable process that ensures your important files are protected without requiring constant manual intervention. In this section, we'll walk you through how to automate the backup process using Python's built-in libraries like `shutil` and `pathlib`.

Why You Should Automate Backups

Many people don't back up their files regularly because it feels like a hassle. You may even do it manually—copying important files to an external hard drive or cloud storage—but these methods can be error-prone, forgettable, and time-consuming.

Automating the backup process with Python offers several advantages:

- **Consistency**: A script can run at regular intervals, ensuring you never forget to back up your files.
- **Efficiency**: Python can back up multiple files, directories, or even entire systems with just a few lines of code.
- **Peace of Mind**: Once your backup system is automated, you no longer have to worry about whether your important files are safely stored.

Let's see how you can implement automatic backups.

Backing Up Files and Folders

A simple backup solution could involve copying files from one location to another. With Python, we can use the `shutil` library to copy files or even entire directories. Here's a basic script that copies all files from a source folder to a backup folder:

```python
import shutil
from pathlib import Path

# Define source and backup directories
source_dir = Path("/Users/you/Documents")
backup_dir = Path("/Users/you/Backups")

# Create backup folder if it doesn't exist
backup_dir.mkdir(parents=True, exist_ok=True)

# Copy all files from source to backup
for file in source_dir.glob("*.*"):
    shutil.copy(file, backup_dir / file.name)

print("Backup completed!")
```

In this script:

- We define `source_dir` and `backup_dir` to specify the directories.

- The `glob("*.*")` method finds all files in the source directory, and `shutil.copy()` copies each one to the backup folder.

This simple approach works well for backing up files that don't change frequently, but it does have some limitations. For instance, it doesn't handle file overwriting or keeping multiple versions of files.

Incremental Backups

A more efficient approach is to only copy files that have changed since the last backup. This process, known as *incremental backup*, ensures that you don't waste time copying files that are already backed up.

Here's an updated version of the script that only copies files modified after a certain date:

```
import shutil
from pathlib import Path
import os
import time

# Define source and backup directories
source_dir = Path("/Users/you/Documents")
backup_dir = Path("/Users/you/Backups")

# Create backup folder if it doesn't exist
backup_dir.mkdir(parents=True, exist_ok=True)

# Get the current time
current_time = time.time()

# Backup only files modified in the last 24 hours
for file in source_dir.glob("*.*"):
    file_mod_time = file.stat().st_mtime
    if current_time - file_mod_time < 86400:  # 86400 seconds
= 24 hours
        shutil.copy(file, backup_dir / file.name)

print("Incremental backup completed!")
```

In this script:

- We use the `st_mtime` attribute to get the last modification time of each file.

40

- The script checks if the file has been modified within the last 24 hours (86400 seconds).
- Only these files are copied to the backup folder, ensuring that you're not backing up files unnecessarily.

This technique reduces the amount of data transferred and speeds up the backup process.

Backing Up and Creating Folder Structure

If you're backing up a whole project or multiple folders, you'll want to maintain the original folder structure in your backup. You can do this with `shutil.copytree()`, which copies entire directories, including subdirectories:

```python
import shutil
from pathlib import Path

# Define source and backup directories
source_dir = Path("/Users/you/Projects")
backup_dir = Path("/Users/you/Backups")

# Create backup folder if it doesn't exist
backup_dir.mkdir(parents=True, exist_ok=True)

# Copy entire source folder to backup location
shutil.copytree(source_dir, backup_dir / source_dir.name)

print(f"Backup of {source_dir.name} completed!")
```

In this case:

- The `copytree()` function copies the entire directory structure, including any nested folders and files.
- The `name` method ensures that the folder is backed up with its original name.

This solution is ideal when you need to back up an entire directory, including subdirectories, and want to preserve the structure for easier access later.

Automating Regular Backups

Once you have your backup script set up, you can automate it to run at regular intervals using Python's `schedule` library, which lets you run the script daily, weekly, or monthly.

Here's a basic script that runs the backup every day at midnight:

```python
import schedule
import time

def backup_files():
    # Add your backup code here (e.g., using shutil)
    print("Backup is running...")

# Schedule the backup to run every day at midnight
schedule.every().day.at("00:00").do(backup_files)

while True:
    schedule.run_pending()
    time.sleep(60)  # Wait for 60 seconds
```

In this case:

- The `schedule` library helps set the backup to run every day at midnight.
- The script runs continuously in the background, checking whether it's time to perform the backup.

With this solution, your backup process is automated without needing to manually run the script every time.

Final Thoughts

Creating file backups is a crucial part of digital organization, and automating this process with Python makes it seamless and reliable. Whether you're backing up files to a different folder, managing incremental backups, or automating regular backups with a scheduler, Python's built-in libraries allow you to protect your data with minimal effort.

2.5 Project: File Organizer Bot

Welcome to the final part of this chapter! Now that we've covered how to automate tasks like organizing files by type, backing up data, and working with the OS using Python, it's time to put all of this into action. In this section, we'll create a **File Organizer Bot** that combines everything we've learned so far into a practical project.

The goal of this project is to build a bot that can:

- Automatically sort files into folders based on file types.
- Rename files in bulk to give them a consistent naming format.
- Create backups of important files.
- Organize files by date or project-specific categories.

By the end of this section, you'll have a working Python bot that can make file organization much more efficient. This bot can easily be extended to fit your specific needs, whether for personal use or within a business setting.

Step 1: Planning the File Organizer Bot

Before jumping into the code, let's first outline what our bot will do. The bot will need to:

- Scan a specified directory for all files.
- Sort those files into subfolders by file type (e.g., `.txt` files go into a "Text Documents" folder, `.jpg` files go into "Images").
- Rename files in bulk if needed, such as adding a prefix or suffix.
- Back up important files regularly.
- Organize files by date or category for more personalized organization.

Step 2: Setting Up the Bot

We will use the libraries we've already introduced (`os`, `shutil`, `pathlib`, and `datetime`) to handle all the necessary tasks. Here's a skeleton of the bot:

```python
import shutil
from pathlib import Path
import datetime
import os
import time

class FileOrganizerBot:
    def __init__(self, source_directory, backup_directory):
        self.source_directory = Path(source_directory)
        self.backup_directory = Path(backup_directory)

    def organize_by_type(self):
        """Organizes files by file type (extension)"""
        file_types = {
            'Images': ['.jpg', '.jpeg', '.png', '.gif'],
            'Documents': ['.pdf', '.docx', '.txt'],
            'Spreadsheets': ['.xlsx', '.csv']
        }

        for file in self.source_directory.glob("*.*"):
            for category, extensions in file_types.items():
                if file.suffix.lower() in extensions:
                    category_folder = self.source_directory / category
                    category_folder.mkdir(exist_ok=True)
                    shutil.move(str(file), category_folder / file.name)
                    break

    def rename_files(self, prefix="File_"):
        """Renames files with a specified prefix"""
        for file in self.source_directory.glob("*.*"):
            new_name = prefix + file.name
            shutil.move(str(file), file.parent / new_name)

    def create_backup(self):
        """Creates a backup of the files"""
        timestamp = datetime.datetime.now().strftime("%Y-%m-%d_%H-%M-%S")
        backup_folder = self.backup_directory / f"backup_{timestamp}"
        backup_folder.mkdir(parents=True, exist_ok=True)

        for file in self.source_directory.glob("*.*"):
            shutil.copy(file, backup_folder / file.name)

    def organize_by_date(self):
        """Organizes files by their last modified date"""
        for file in self.source_directory.glob("*.*"):
            mod_time = datetime.datetime.fromtimestamp(file.stat().st_mtime)
```

```python
            year_month = f"{mod_time.year}-
{mod_time.month:02}"

            date_folder = self.source_directory / year_month
            date_folder.mkdir(exist_ok=True)
            shutil.move(str(file), date_folder / file.name)

    def run(self):
        """Runs the entire file organization process"""
        print("Organizing files by type...")
        self.organize_by_type()
        print("Renaming files...")
        self.rename_files()
        print("Creating backup...")
        self.create_backup()
        print("Organizing files by date...")
        self.organize_by_date()

        print("File organization complete!")
if __name__ == "__main__":
    source_dir = "/path/to/your/source/folder"
    backup_dir = "/path/to/your/backup/folder"
    bot = FileOrganizerBot(source_dir, backup_dir)
    bot.run()
```

Step 3: Code Breakdown

Let's break down what each part of this script is doing:

- **The `FileOrganizerBot` Class**: This is where all the core functions of the bot are contained. The bot's main task is to organize, rename, back up, and categorize files. The class takes two arguments when instantiated: `source_directory` (the folder where files are stored) and `backup_directory` (where the backups will be saved).
- **Organizing by File Type (`organize_by_type`)**: This function sorts files into subfolders based on their file extension. For example, `.jpg` files are moved into an "Images" folder. You can easily modify the `file_types` dictionary to add or remove categories based on your needs.
- **Renaming Files (`rename_files`)**: Here, you can specify a prefix (like `"File_"`) that will be added to the beginning of each file's name. You can modify this to also add suffixes or even date stamps.
- **Creating Backups (`create_backup`)**: This function makes a backup of all the files in the source directory and saves them in the backup

45

folder. It adds a timestamp to each backup to keep different versions organized.

- **Organizing by Date (`organize_by_date`)**: Files are grouped based on their last modified date (e.g., 2023-04, 2023-05). This helps keep files organized chronologically.
- **Running the Bot (`run`)**: This function calls all of the functions in sequence: organizing by type, renaming, backing up, and organizing by date.

Step 4: Running the File Organizer Bot

To run the bot, you just need to update the paths to your source and backup directories and then execute the script. The bot will perform the following tasks:

1. Organize the files in your source folder by type (images, documents, etc.).
2. Rename all files by adding the specified prefix.
3. Create a backup of the files in the backup folder, naming the backup by the current timestamp.
4. Organize files in the source directory by their last modified date.

Once the bot has finished running, your files will be neatly organized in their respective folders, and you'll have a backup ready to go in case of any emergencies.

Step 5: Customizing the Bot

The File Organizer Bot is designed to be flexible and can be easily customized:

- You can modify the file types and backup structure to fit your specific needs.
- You could add additional features, like organizing files by project name or moving files based on custom naming conventions.
- You might want to add error handling or logging to track any issues during execution.

Final Thoughts

Building a **File Organizer Bot** is a great way to automate mundane tasks like file sorting and backups. With just a few lines of Python code, you can save time, reduce the risk of human error, and ensure that your files are always organized and backed up properly.

By now, you should feel comfortable with the process of automating file management tasks using Python. You can now take this bot and expand upon it, creating a solution that fits your specific use case. Whether you need to organize thousands of files, create regular backups, or even sort files based on their contents, Python is an excellent tool to get the job done.

Chapter 3: Web Scraping and Automation

In the world of automation, **web scraping** is one of the most powerful tools at your disposal. Whether you're gathering data for analysis, automating repetitive web tasks, or even just pulling in information to make your life easier, web scraping can save you countless hours.

In this chapter, we will dive into the basics of web scraping, using Python's robust libraries like `requests`, `BeautifulSoup`, and `selenium`. By the end, you'll know how to scrape data from websites, handle forms and sessions, and even automate browser actions.

Let's get started!

3.1 Introduction to Requests and BeautifulSoup

In the world of web scraping, **Requests** and **BeautifulSoup** are two of the most commonly used Python libraries. Together, they form the foundation of most scraping tasks. If you're new to web scraping, don't worry! I'll guide you step-by-step, so you can learn how to pull data from websites with ease.

Before diving into how these tools work, let's take a moment to understand the overall process of web scraping. Web scraping involves fetching data from a website (usually HTML data) and extracting useful information from it. Think of it as reading through a webpage and picking out the parts that are interesting or useful to you—whether that's job listings, book titles, or the latest product prices.

Now, let's break down how **Requests** and **BeautifulSoup** help us achieve this.

What is Requests?

The **Requests** library is the go-to Python tool for sending HTTP requests to retrieve content from websites. When you visit a webpage in your browser, it sends an HTTP request to the web server, which responds with HTML (or other content). The same thing happens in Python with Requests. You send a request to the website's server, and the server responds with the content you requested.

One of the reasons Requests is so popular is its simplicity. You don't need to worry about all the low-level details like handling cookies or managing connection timeouts—Requests takes care of all of that for you.

Here's a quick example of how you can use Requests to get the content of a webpage:

```
import requests

# Define the URL of the page you want to scrape
url = 'https://quotes.toscrape.com'

# Send a GET request to the website
response = requests.get(url)

# Check if the request was successful
if response.status_code == 200:
    print('Page successfully fetched!')
    print(response.text)  # Print the HTML content of the
page
else:
    print(f"Failed to retrieve the page. Status code:
{response.status_code}")
```

In this code:

- We use `requests.get(url)` to send a GET request to the URL.
- If the request is successful (`status_code == 200`), we print out the raw HTML of the page using `response.text`.
- If the request fails (maybe the website is down or the URL is wrong), we print the error code.

What is BeautifulSoup?

While Requests fetches the raw HTML content of a page, **BeautifulSoup** comes in to help you **parse** and **extract** meaningful data from it. The HTML response is often messy and filled with tags, but BeautifulSoup makes it easy to navigate this structure and pick out the information you care about.

With BeautifulSoup, you can:

- Find specific elements (like headings, links, paragraphs, or images).
- Extract text from within HTML tags.
- Navigate the HTML structure easily.

To install **BeautifulSoup**, you need to install it alongside a parser (usually `html.parser` or `lxml`). Here's how you can install it:

```
pip install beautifulsoup4
```

Once installed, you can use it to parse the HTML content fetched by Requests.

Here's a simple example of using BeautifulSoup:

```
from bs4 import BeautifulSoup

# Get the HTML content (using the response from the earlier
example)
html_content = response.text

# Parse the HTML with BeautifulSoup
soup = BeautifulSoup(html_content, 'html.parser')

# Find all quotes on the page
quotes = soup.find_all('span', class_='text')

# Print each quote
for quote in quotes:
    print(quote.get_text())
```

In this code:

- We use `BeautifulSoup(response.text, 'html.parser')` to parse the HTML content that we retrieved using Requests.

- The `find_all()` method is used to find all the `<span>` tags with a class of `text` (where the quotes are located).
- We loop through each quote and extract just the text inside the span tag using `quote.get_text()`.

Why Should You Use Requests and BeautifulSoup Together?

While Requests alone can fetch the raw HTML content of a webpage, it's BeautifulSoup that makes that content **understandable** and **useful**. Think of it this way: **Requests** gets you the page; **BeautifulSoup** helps you extract the data you actually care about from the page. Without both, you would end up with raw HTML that's hard to process or use.

Imagine you want to scrape job listings from a website. You could use Requests to get the HTML of the page, but then you would need a tool to dig through that HTML and extract job titles, locations, and descriptions. BeautifulSoup is perfect for this.

How to Choose Between `requests` and `BeautifulSoup`

- **Requests**: Used to **retrieve** data from the web.
- **BeautifulSoup**: Used to **parse** and **extract** specific elements from the HTML.

Think of them as a two-step process: **Requests** first brings in the raw data, and then **BeautifulSoup** helps you make sense of it.

Handling Errors and Edge Cases

When web scraping, things don't always go as planned. Websites might be down, your request might be blocked, or the structure of the HTML might change. Here are a couple of things to keep in mind when using Requests and BeautifulSoup:

- **Check Response Codes**: Always check if the page was fetched successfully by looking at the HTTP response code. A successful

51

request has a status code of `200`. If you get `404`, that means the page doesn't exist; if it's `403`, your request may have been blocked.
- **Handle Exceptions**: Sometimes, your requests might time out or fail for other reasons. It's good practice to handle such errors gracefully.

Here's how you can handle errors when making requests:

```
try:
    response = requests.get('https://quotes.toscrape.com')
    response.raise_for_status()  # Raise an exception for
HTTP errors
    print('Page successfully fetched!')
except requests.exceptions.RequestException as e:
    print(f"Error: {e}")
```

In this example:

- `response.raise_for_status()` will raise an exception if the status code is not `200`, which helps us catch errors like `404` or `403`.
- `requests.exceptions.RequestException` is a general exception that catches all errors related to the request.

The Power of Combining Requests and BeautifulSoup

When combined, **Requests** and **BeautifulSoup** allow you to scrape data, parse it, and extract meaningful information from websites with minimal code. Together, they open up a whole new world of automation and data extraction possibilities.

The next step is to apply these skills to real-world scraping projects, such as scraping job listings, product prices, or even news headlines.

3.2 Extracting Data from Websites

Once you've learned how to use **Requests** to fetch a webpage and **BeautifulSoup** to parse the HTML, the next step is to actually **extract** meaningful data from the page. Whether you're scraping job listings, product details, or news headlines, the goal is to pinpoint exactly where the information you need resides and extract it cleanly.

In this guide, we'll break down the process of extracting data from websites in a way that's easy to understand, with a focus on making sure you know how to select the correct elements and retrieve the data you want.

Understanding the HTML Structure

To successfully extract data, it's essential to first understand the **structure** of the HTML content you're working with. Think of HTML as a **tree structure**, where each piece of data is nested within specific tags. Each tag can have attributes (like `class`, `id`, or `href`) that define its characteristics.

Here's an example of what part of the HTML of a job listing page might look like:

```
<div class="job-listing">
    <h2 class="job-title">Software Engineer</h2>
    <p class="company">Tech Corp</p>
    <p class="location">San Francisco, CA</p>
    <a href="https://example.com/job/1234" class="apply-
link">Apply Now</a>
</div>
```

In this example, the **job title** is inside an `<h2>` tag with the class `job-title`, the **company** is inside a `<p>` tag with the class `company`, and the **location** is in a `<p>` tag with the class `location`. These tags and classes are our targets for extracting data.

Extracting Data with BeautifulSoup

Now, let's dive into the actual extraction process using BeautifulSoup. After fetching the webpage and parsing it, you'll use **BeautifulSoup's methods** to search for and select the elements containing the data you want.

Here's how to extract specific elements like the job title, company name, and location from the HTML structure above:

```
from bs4 import BeautifulSoup
import requests

# Step 1: Fetch the page content
```

```
url = 'https://example.com/job-listings'
response = requests.get(url)
soup = BeautifulSoup(response.text, 'html.parser')

# Step 2: Extract job listings
job_listings = soup.find_all('div', class_='job-listing')

# Step 3: Loop through each job listing and extract details
for job in job_listings:
    title = job.find('h2', class_='job-title').get_text()   #
Extract job title
    company = job.find('p', class_='company').get_text()     #
Extract company name
    location = job.find('p', class_='location').get_text() #
Extract job location

    # Print extracted information
    print(f"Job Title: {title}")
    print(f"Company: {company}")
    print(f"Location: {location}")
    print('---')
```

Breaking Down the Code

- **find_all()**: This method is used to find all instances of a given tag with a specific class. In this case, we're looking for all div elements with the class job-listing, which each represent a single job.
- **find()**: Once we have a job_listing, we use find() to retrieve specific elements within that job listing, such as the title, company, and location. For example, job.find('h2', class_='job-title') locates the h2 tag inside each div with the class job-listing.
- **.get_text()**: This method extracts just the **text content** from an HTML element, removing any HTML tags. For instance, job.find('h2', class_='job-title').get_text() gives us the job title without any extra HTML code.

Using Different Selectors to Target Specific Elements

One of the most powerful features of BeautifulSoup is the flexibility in how you can target elements. There are several ways to find the elements you need depending on the structure of the webpage.

- **Finding by Tag**: You can search by the tag name, like `'h1'`, `'a'`, or `'div'`.

  ```
  title = soup.find('h2').get_text()
  ```

- **Finding by Class**: As we've seen, you can also target elements by their class. This is especially helpful when the same type of data (like job listings) is repeated across multiple elements on a page.

  ```
  company = soup.find('p', class_='company').get_text()
  ```

- **Finding by ID**: If the element has an `id` attribute, you can find it directly by ID.

  ```
  header = soup.find(id='main-header').get_text()
  ```

- **Using CSS Selectors**: BeautifulSoup also supports CSS selectors, which give you more power to select complex nested elements.

  ```
  links = soup.select('div.job-listing > a')  # Find all
  links within a job listing
  ```

This flexibility allows you to navigate HTML like an expert and pull out exactly what you need, regardless of how the webpage is structured.

Dealing with Multiple Pages

In many cases, the data you want isn't just on one page; it's spread across multiple pages, often with a "Next" button or pagination system. You can scrape data across multiple pages by finding the "Next" button's link and sending requests to each subsequent page.

Here's an example of scraping data across multiple pages:

```
page_number = 1
while True:
    url = f'https://example.com/jobs?page={page_number}'
    response = requests.get(url)
    soup = BeautifulSoup(response.text, 'html.parser')

    job_listings = soup.find_all('div', class_='job-listing')
    if not job_listings:
```

```
        break  # Exit the loop if there are no more job
listings

    for job in job_listings:
        title = job.find('h2', class_='job-title').get_text()
        company = job.find('p', class_='company').get_text()
        location = job.find('p',
class_='location').get_text()
        print(f"Job Title: {title}\nCompany:
{company}\nLocation: {location}")

    page_number += 1   # Move to the next page
```

In this code:

- We loop through pages by incrementing `page_number` in the URL.
- The loop stops when there are no more job listings on the page.

Handling Missing or Empty Data

Not every webpage will structure its HTML in the same way, and not every job listing will have all the information you're looking for. Sometimes, a job listing might be missing a title, a company name, or a location. When scraping, you should always **handle these cases** gracefully to avoid errors in your code.

You can use a `try-except` block or simply check if an element exists before extracting it:

```
for job in job_listings:
    title = job.find('h2', class_='job-title')
    company = job.find('p', class_='company')
    location = job.find('p', class_='location')

    # Check if any element is missing and handle accordingly
    if title:
        title = title.get_text()
    else:
        title = 'No title available'

    if company:
        company = company.get_text()
    else:
        company = 'No company available'
```

```
if location:
    location = location.get_text()
else:
    location = 'No location available'

print(f"Job Title: {title}")
print(f"Company: {company}")
print(f"Location: {location}")
print('---')
```

Conclusion

Extracting data from websites with **BeautifulSoup** and **Requests** is a crucial skill for anyone who wants to automate the process of gathering information from the web. By understanding the structure of HTML, using selectors like `find()` and `find_all()`, and handling common edge cases like missing data, you can build powerful scraping tools that save time and effort.

3.3 Handling Web Forms and Sessions

When automating tasks on the web, you'll often encounter forms. Forms can be used for anything from logging into a website to searching for specific items, submitting user data, or navigating pages. In this section, we'll explore how to handle web forms and maintain sessions using **Requests** and **BeautifulSoup**. We'll also discuss how sessions work and how to manage them effectively for more complex scraping tasks.

What are Web Forms and Why Do They Matter?

Web forms are a fundamental part of most interactive websites. They allow users to input data that gets sent to the server. This can be through:

- **Login forms** where users enter their credentials.
- **Search forms** where you submit a query and retrieve results.
- **Subscription forms** for newsletters or other signups.

For web scraping, interacting with forms often means submitting data to a server and capturing the results, just like you would manually fill out a form in a browser.

In Python, the **Requests** library makes it easy to work with forms, while **BeautifulSoup** can help parse any results.

Making a POST Request to Submit a Form

When you fill out and submit a form on a website, you're usually sending data to the server via a **POST** request. In this case, we simulate the form submission using the **Requests** library.

Let's walk through an example. Imagine we want to log into a website. Here's what a typical login form might look like in HTML:

```
<form action="/login" method="POST">
    <input type="text" name="username"
placeholder="Username">
    <input type="password" name="password"
placeholder="Password">
    <input type="submit" value="Login">
</form>
```

In this form:

- The **action** attribute tells us where the form data is sent (`/login`).
- The **method** is **POST**, meaning the form data will be submitted in the request body, not in the URL.
- The **name** attributes of the `<input>` tags (`username`, `password`) are the keys we'll use to send data in the request.

To simulate submitting this form in Python:

```
import requests

# URL of the login form
login_url = 'https://example.com/login'

# Data we want to send in the POST request
login_data = {
    'username': 'myUsername',
    'password': 'myPassword'
```

```
}

# Make the POST request
response = requests.post(login_url, data=login_data)

# Check if the login was successful
if response.ok:
    print("Login successful!")
else:
    print("Login failed!")
```

In this code:

- We use `requests.post()` to send data to the login URL.
- The **login_data** dictionary holds the form's data, where the keys match the **name** attributes of the form fields (`username`, `password`).
- After sending the POST request, we check the **status of the response** using `response.ok` to see if the login was successful.

Handling Sessions: Keeping Track of Login States

Websites often require that once you log in, you maintain your session so you don't need to log in again for every subsequent request. This is typically done through **cookies** or **session IDs**. The **Requests** library provides a great way to manage these sessions with the **Session** object.

A **session** in Requests stores cookies across multiple requests, which allows you to persist login credentials and other data. Here's how you can use a session to handle multiple requests after logging in:

```
import requests

# Create a session object
session = requests.Session()

# Data for logging in
login_data = {
    'username': 'myUsername',
    'password': 'myPassword'
}

# Send login request
login_url = 'https://example.com/login'
session.post(login_url, data=login_data)
```

```
# Now you can use the session to make subsequent requests
dashboard_url = 'https://example.com/dashboard'
response = session.get(dashboard_url)

# Check if we're logged in
if response.ok:
    print("Accessing dashboard successfully!")
else:
    print("Failed to access dashboard!")
```

In this example:

- We create a `session` object using `requests.Session()`.
- The session object allows us to automatically send the **cookies** from the login request with every subsequent request.
- After logging in, we use the same session to access another page (`/dashboard`), keeping the login session active.

Working with Web Forms for Search and Other Submissions

Forms aren't just for logging in. You may want to interact with other types of forms, such as search forms or data submission forms. For example, a search form may look like this:

```
<form action="/search" method="GET">
    <input type="text" name="query" placeholder="Search">
    <input type="submit" value="Search">
</form>
```

In this case, the search form sends a **GET** request with a query parameter. Here's how you can automate a search using Python:

```
import requests

# URL for the search form
search_url = 'https://example.com/search'

# Search term to send in the GET request
search_data = {'query': 'python automation'}

# Send the GET request with the search query
response = requests.get(search_url, params=search_data)
```

60

```
# Print the results
if response.ok:
    print("Search successful!")
    print(response.text)  # Display the raw HTML response
(for now)
else:
    print("Search failed!")
```

This script:

- Sends a **GET** request to the search URL with a `query` parameter.
- The `params` argument in `requests.get()` adds the search term (`'python automation'`) as a query string in the URL (like `?query=python+automation`).
- Finally, it prints the response from the server (which, depending on the website, could be an HTML page with search results).

Dealing with Captchas and Other Anti-Scraping Measures

A common challenge when working with web forms is dealing with **CAPTCHAs**—those tests that verify you're not a bot. While bypassing CAPTCHAs goes beyond the scope of this book, it's important to note that many websites employ such measures to prevent scraping. If you encounter a CAPTCHA, the best course of action is to explore whether the website provides an API for data access, which is typically a more reliable and legal method.

Conclusion

Handling web forms and maintaining sessions are crucial parts of web scraping. With **Requests** and **BeautifulSoup**, you can simulate form submissions, keep track of login sessions across multiple requests, and interact with websites in ways that mirror real user behavior. This opens up many possibilities, from logging in and accessing account data to automating searches and form submissions.

3.4 Automating Browsers with Selenium

While **Requests** and **BeautifulSoup** are fantastic for scraping static websites, they have limitations when dealing with dynamic content—pages that load their data through JavaScript. In such cases, **Selenium** becomes a powerful tool. It allows you to interact with a real web browser, simulating actions like clicks, scrolling, and filling out forms, just as a human user would.

Selenium can open a browser, click buttons, extract data, and even wait for JavaScript to load content, all of which makes it indispensable for scraping complex, dynamic websites.

What is Selenium?

Selenium is a browser automation tool, originally designed for testing web applications. Over time, it has become a go-to tool for automating browsers to scrape and interact with websites. It controls a web browser in the same way a human user would, making it ideal for scraping sites where data is generated dynamically by JavaScript.

With Selenium, you can:

- Open websites in real browsers like Chrome or Firefox.
- Navigate through websites by simulating mouse movements and keyboard input.
- Wait for elements to load before interacting with them.
- Scrape content rendered by JavaScript, which is not possible with **Requests** alone.

Setting Up Selenium

Before diving into coding with Selenium, let's set up the environment. You'll need:

- **Selenium WebDriver**: This is the core of Selenium, which allows Python to communicate with the browser.

- **WebDriver for your browser**: For instance, ChromeDriver for Google Chrome or geckodriver for Firefox.

1. Install Selenium

You can install Selenium using **pip**, the Python package manager:

```
pip install selenium
```

2. Download a WebDriver

If you plan to use **Google Chrome**, you'll need **ChromeDriver**.

Ensure that you download the version of ChromeDriver that matches your browser version.

After downloading, extract the driver to a location on your computer. You'll need to point Selenium to this driver in your code.

Getting Started with Selenium: Opening a Web Browser

Once you've installed Selenium and downloaded the appropriate WebDriver, you're ready to open a web browser. Let's begin with opening Google Chrome:

```python
from selenium import webdriver

# Path to the ChromeDriver (adjust this if necessary)
driver_path = '/path/to/chromedriver'

# Launch a new instance of Chrome
driver = webdriver.Chrome(executable_path=driver_path)

# Open a website
driver.get('https://www.example.com')

# Close the browser once we're done
driver.quit()
```

This code opens a new Chrome window and navigates to "example.com". Once the script finishes, it closes the browser with `driver.quit()`.

Interacting with Web Elements

A huge advantage of using Selenium is that it can interact with any web element on a page. Whether it's a button, text field, or dropdown, Selenium can simulate user input.

Here's an example where we search on Google:

```python
from selenium import webdriver
from selenium.webdriver.common.keys import Keys

# Path to the ChromeDriver
driver_path = '/path/to/chromedriver'
driver = webdriver.Chrome(executable_path=driver_path)

# Open Google
driver.get("https://www.google.com")

# Find the search input field by its name attribute
search_box = driver.find_element_by_name("q")

# Type a query and submit it
search_box.send_keys("Python Automation")
search_box.send_keys(Keys.RETURN)

# Wait for a few seconds (optional, to see the results)
import time
time.sleep(3)

# Close the browser
driver.quit()
```

In this example:

- We use `find_element_by_name()` to locate the search box by its **name** attribute (`q`).
- We use `send_keys()` to type our search query ("Python Automation") into the search box.
- Finally, we use `Keys.RETURN` to simulate pressing the **Enter** key, which submits the search.

Waiting for Elements to Load

One of the common issues when automating browsers is that the content may take some time to load, especially if the page is dynamic (i.e., it loads data via JavaScript after the initial page load). Selenium offers **waits**, which allow your script to pause until an element is present on the page or a certain condition is met.

There are two main types of waits in Selenium:

- **Implicit Wait**: This tells Selenium to wait for a certain amount of time before throwing an error if the element isn't found.
- **Explicit Wait**: This allows you to wait for a specific condition to be true before proceeding, like waiting for an element to be clickable.

Here's an example using **Explicit Wait** to wait for an element to become visible before interacting with it:

```
from selenium import webdriver
from selenium.webdriver.common.by import By
from selenium.webdriver.support.ui import WebDriverWait
from selenium.webdriver.support import expected_conditions as
EC

driver_path = '/path/to/chromedriver'
driver = webdriver.Chrome(executable_path=driver_path)

# Open a website
driver.get('https://www.example.com')

# Wait for a specific element to become clickable
wait = WebDriverWait(driver, 10)  # Wait up to 10 seconds
button = wait.until(EC.element_to_be_clickable((By.ID,
'submit_button')))

# Click the button once it's clickable
button.click()

# Close the browser
driver.quit()
```

In this example:

- `WebDriverWait(driver, 10)` waits for up to 10 seconds for the element to become available.

- `EC.element_to_be_clickable((By.ID, 'submit_button'))` specifies the condition we are waiting for: the button to become clickable.
- Once the condition is met, we interact with the button by calling `button.click()`.

Extracting Data from Dynamic Content

One of the biggest reasons to use Selenium is to scrape content that's dynamically loaded with JavaScript. After you simulate a click or interact with a page, you can extract the page source and use **BeautifulSoup** to parse it, just like you would with static HTML.

For example, let's say you want to scrape the titles of job listings from a dynamically loaded page:

```
from selenium import webdriver
from bs4 import BeautifulSoup

driver_path = '/path/to/chromedriver'
driver = webdriver.Chrome(executable_path=driver_path)

# Open the job listings page
driver.get('https://www.example.com/jobs')

# Wait for the job listings to load
driver.implicitly_wait(5)

# Get the page source after the JavaScript has loaded the
content
page_source = driver.page_source

# Parse the page source with BeautifulSoup
soup = BeautifulSoup(page_source, 'html.parser')

# Extract and print job titles
job_titles = soup.find_all('h2', class_='job-title')
for title in job_titles:
    print(title.get_text())

# Close the browser
driver.quit()
```

Here:

- We use `driver.page_source` to get the full HTML content of the page, including the dynamically loaded elements.
- BeautifulSoup is used to parse the HTML, and then we extract the job titles by searching for all `<h2>` elements with the class `'job-title'`.

Conclusion

Selenium opens up a world of possibilities for web scraping when it comes to handling dynamic content. By automating browsers, you can interact with websites like a human user, handling everything from clicking buttons to filling out forms and waiting for content to load.

With this power at your disposal, you can scrape even the most complex sites, extract the data you need, and automate tasks that would be nearly impossible with just Requests or BeautifulSoup alone.

3.5 Project: Job Listing Scraper

Now that you have a solid understanding of web scraping with **Selenium** and **BeautifulSoup**, it's time to put everything together in a practical project. We'll build a **Job Listing Scraper** that can automatically scrape job postings from a website and save them into a structured format, such as a CSV file.

This project will showcase how to:

- Navigate through dynamic websites.
- Extract relevant information (like job titles, company names, and locations).
- Store the data in a readable format for future use.

Let's get started!

Choosing the Website

For this project, we'll use a hypothetical job listing website. The principles, however, will apply to any job listing site, such as **Indeed**, **LinkedIn**, or **Glassdoor**.

Before we dive into coding, let's define the data we want to collect. Typical job listings contain:

- Job title
- Company name
- Location
- Job description or link to more details

We'll use **Selenium** to open the page, simulate scrolling (if necessary), and **BeautifulSoup** to parse the content.

Step 1: Setting Up Your Environment

First, ensure you have the necessary libraries installed. If you haven't already, install **Selenium** and **BeautifulSoup** using **pip**:

```
pip install selenium beautifulsoup4 pandas
```

Next, ensure you have downloaded the appropriate **WebDriver** for your browser (ChromeDriver for Chrome, geckodriver for Firefox, etc.).

Step 2: Navigating to the Website

We begin by opening the website with **Selenium**. Let's say we are scraping job listings from a website like **examplejobs.com**. The website has a list of job postings, and we'll navigate through multiple pages if needed.

Here's the first step:

```
from selenium import webdriver
from selenium.webdriver.common.by import By
from selenium.webdriver.common.keys import Keys
```

```
import time

# Set up the driver (adjust path to your WebDriver)
driver_path = '/path/to/chromedriver'
driver = webdriver.Chrome(executable_path=driver_path)

# Open the job listings website
driver.get("https://www.examplejobs.com")

# Wait for the page to load
time.sleep(3)  # Adjust the sleep time based on your internet
speed
```

This code opens the website and waits a few seconds to ensure that the page has loaded completely.

Step 3: Scrolling and Waiting for Dynamic Content

Many job listing sites load content dynamically (e.g., as you scroll down the page). To deal with this, we can simulate scrolling to trigger the loading of new job posts.

Here's how to scroll down the page:

```
# Scroll down to load more content (simulating user behavior)
for _ in range(3):  # Adjust the number of times you want to
scroll
    driver.execute_script("window.scrollTo(0,
document.body.scrollHeight);")
    time.sleep(2)  # Wait for new content to load
```

This script scrolls down the page three times and waits 2 seconds after each scroll to let the content load.

Step 4: Extracting Job Data with BeautifulSoup

Once we've scrolled down and the page is loaded, it's time to extract the job data. We'll use **BeautifulSoup** to parse the page source and extract the job titles, company names, and locations.

Let's define the job details we want to extract:

```
from bs4 import BeautifulSoup

# Get the page source after dynamic content has loaded
page_source = driver.page_source
soup = BeautifulSoup(page_source, 'html.parser')

# Find all the job posting elements
job_elements = soup.find_all('div', class_='job-listing')  #
Adjust the class name based on the site
```

Here, `job-listing` is just a placeholder class name for the job posts. You'll need to inspect the HTML of your chosen website to find the appropriate tag and class names.

Step 5: Extracting Specific Details

Now, we'll extract the specific details for each job posting. Let's assume that each job listing has the following structure:

- A job title inside an `<h2>` tag.
- The company name in a `<span>` tag with the class `'company-name'`.
- The job location in a `<span>` tag with the class `'job-location'`.

Let's extract this information:

```
jobs = []

for job in job_elements:
    title = job.find('h2').get_text(strip=True)
    company = job.find('span', class_='company-
name').get_text(strip=True)
    location = job.find('span', class_='job-
location').get_text(strip=True)

    jobs.append({
        'Title': title,
        'Company': company,
        'Location': location
    })
```

Here, we use `.get_text(strip=True)` to remove any extra whitespace around the text.

Step 6: Saving the Data to a CSV File

Once we have all the job data, the next step is to save it into a structured format like a **CSV file**. We'll use the **Pandas** library to do this efficiently.

First, install **Pandas** if you haven't already:

```
pip install pandas
```

Then, we can write the job data into a CSV file:

```
import pandas as pd

# Convert the list of dictionaries into a DataFrame
df = pd.DataFrame(jobs)

# Save the DataFrame to a CSV file
df.to_csv('job_listings.csv', index=False)

print("Job listings saved to 'job_listings.csv'.")
```

This will create a CSV file named **job_listings.csv** with the columns **Title**, **Company**, and **Location**, containing the data you scraped.

Step 7: Closing the Browser

Once you've completed the scraping, make sure to close the browser to free up resources.

```
# Close the browser
driver.quit()
```

Final Thoughts

By combining **Selenium** and **BeautifulSoup**, we can scrape dynamic content and save valuable data from job listing sites. This project has given us the tools to automate data extraction from websites that load content with JavaScript, something that's difficult to handle with just static scraping tools like **Requests**.

Remember, scraping websites comes with ethical and legal considerations:

- Always respect a site's **robots.txt** file to ensure you're not violating any rules.
- Avoid overloading websites with too many requests in a short period. Implement delays where needed.

Chapter 4: Automating Emails and Messaging

In today's fast-paced world, sending and receiving emails, as well as messages, are part of almost everyone's daily routine. What if you could automate these tasks? Imagine sending automated email reports, scheduling notifications, or even integrating messaging platforms like WhatsApp and Telegram into your workflow. In this chapter, we will explore how Python can help you automate emails and messaging, enabling you to save time and streamline communication.

By the end of this chapter, you'll be able to:

- Send and receive emails automatically.
- Work with email templates and attachments.
- Use messaging APIs like WhatsApp and Telegram for automated notifications.
- Build a useful project—a daily email reporter.

Let's dive in!

4.1 Sending Emails with smtplib

Sending emails through Python might seem like a daunting task at first, but it's quite straightforward once you understand how to use the right libraries. One of the most widely used libraries for sending emails in Python is **smtplib**, which provides an interface to send emails using the **Simple Mail Transfer Protocol (SMTP)**. SMTP is the protocol used by email servers to send mail to other email servers and clients.

In this guide, we'll walk through the process of sending emails using Python's `smtplib`. We'll cover how to connect to an SMTP server, create an email, and send it. Along the way, we'll explain some key concepts and share practical code examples.

Let's get started!

Understanding SMTP and smtplib

Before we dive into the code, it's important to understand a little bit about **SMTP**. SMTP is essentially the backbone for sending emails on the internet. When you send an email using a service like Gmail, Yahoo, or Outlook, it's typically sent via an SMTP server.

Python's `smtplib` module allows you to communicate with SMTP servers and send emails programmatically. It's simple to use and can be integrated into automation scripts where sending emails is part of the task.

Setting Up the SMTP Server

The first thing you need is access to an SMTP server. In this example, we'll use **Gmail's SMTP server**, but you can apply the same principles to other email providers by simply using their respective SMTP server settings.

For Gmail, the SMTP server address is: `smtp.gmail.com`, and it typically operates on **port 465** (SSL) or **port 587** (TLS).

Let's start by connecting to the Gmail SMTP server:

```python
import smtplib

# Sender's email credentials
sender_email = "your_email@gmail.com"
sender_password = "your_email_password"

# Set up the SMTP server (Gmail's SMTP server)
server = smtplib.SMTP_SSL('smtp.gmail.com', 465)  # Using SSL
for secure connection

# Log in to the email server
server.login(sender_email, sender_password)
```

In the code above:

- **SMTP_SSL()** is used to create a secure connection with the SMTP server using SSL encryption.
- **server.login()** logs you into the server using the email credentials provided. This is crucial because the server needs to verify that the user sending the email is authenticated.

Creating the Email Content

Now that we're connected to the SMTP server, let's create the email. To do this, we'll use Python's **email.mime** module, which makes it easy to create both simple and complex email messages.

We'll use the **MIMEMultipart** class to handle multi-part emails (emails that contain both plain text and HTML or attachments). In most cases, even a simple email requires a MIMEMultipart object to handle the structure of the message properly.

```python
from email.mime.multipart import MIMEMultipart
from email.mime.text import MIMEText

# Create the email message
msg = MIMEMultipart()
msg['From'] = sender_email
msg['To'] = "recipient_email@example.com"  # Replace with the
recipient's email address
msg['Subject'] = "Test Email from Python"

# Add the body of the email
body = "Hello, this is a test email sent from Python using
smtplib!"
msg.attach(MIMEText(body, 'plain'))
```

In the code above:

- **MIMEMultipart()** creates a container for the email message.
- **msg['From']** and **msg['To']** are used to specify the sender and recipient addresses.
- **msg['Subject']** specifies the subject of the email.
- **MIMEText()** attaches the email body as plain text. If you wanted to send HTML content, you would pass 'html' instead of 'plain'.

Sending the Email

Once the email message is ready, the next step is to send it. This is done using the **sendmail()** function provided by smtplib.

```python
# Send the email
server.sendmail(sender_email, "recipient_email@example.com",
msg.as_string())
```

The `sendmail()` function sends the email to the specified recipient. The `msg.as_string()` method converts the email object into a format that can be sent over the network.

Closing the Connection

Once the email is sent, it's important to close the server connection properly to free up resources.

```
# Close the connection to the server
server.quit()
```

This ensures that your connection to the SMTP server is closed cleanly.

Handling Authentication Issues

When sending emails via Gmail, it's crucial to be aware of potential authentication issues. For example, Gmail may block sign-ins from less secure apps. To resolve this, you can:

1. Enable **Less Secure App Access** in your Google account settings, but this is not recommended due to security concerns.
2. Use **OAuth2** for more secure authentication.

Alternatively, for better security and ease of use, consider using **App Passwords**. If you have two-factor authentication enabled on your Google account, you can generate a special app password that works exclusively for SMTP, which is a safer option.

To generate an app password in Gmail:

- Go to your **Google Account Settings**.
- Under **Security**, look for **App passwords**.
- Generate a password for the app you are using (in this case, Python).

Use this app password in place of your regular Gmail password when logging into the SMTP server.

Handling Errors and Debugging

It's important to handle errors gracefully when sending emails, especially when working with external services like Gmail. If there's an issue with the connection, authentication, or any other part of the process, you'll want to catch the error and log it for further inspection.

Here's a simple way to handle errors:

```
try:
    # Send the email
    server.sendmail(sender_email,
"recipient_email@example.com", msg.as_string())
    print("Email sent successfully!")

except Exception as e:
    print(f"Error: {e}")

finally:
    # Close the server connection
    server.quit()
```

In this code:

- The **try-except** block ensures that if something goes wrong, the error is caught and displayed.
- The **finally** block ensures that the server connection is always closed, even if an error occurs.

Conclusion

Sending emails using Python and smtplib is relatively simple once you break down the process into clear steps: connect to the SMTP server, create the email message, send the message, and close the connection. By mastering these basics, you can start automating email notifications, reports, and a variety of other tasks that involve email communication.

As you continue learning Python automation, this foundational skill will serve as a stepping stone for more complex projects, like sending automated reminders or integrating emails into larger workflows.

4.2 Reading Emails with imaplib

Reading emails programmatically is a powerful feature that many Python developers leverage for automating tasks such as inbox monitoring, parsing emails for specific content, or triggering other actions based on received messages. While sending emails is great, there are numerous scenarios where retrieving and processing incoming emails becomes essential. For these tasks, Python provides the `imaplib` library, which allows you to interact with email servers via the **IMAP (Internet Message Access Protocol)**.

In this section, we will walk you through how to read emails using Python's `imaplib` library, which provides functionality for connecting to an IMAP server, searching for messages, and extracting email data like subject, sender, body, and attachments.

Understanding IMAP and imaplib

IMAP is a protocol that email clients use to access messages on a mail server. It allows you to retrieve emails without downloading them to your local machine, making it an ideal choice for managing your inbox programmatically. IMAP provides several advantages over POP3 (Post Office Protocol), one of the main differences being that IMAP lets you keep your emails on the server, while POP3 typically downloads and deletes them.

Python's `imaplib` is the module used for interacting with IMAP email servers. It provides methods to connect to a server, authenticate, retrieve email data, and even mark emails as read or delete them.

In this guide, we'll use **Gmail's IMAP server** to demonstrate how to connect to the email service, retrieve emails, and parse their content. The steps, however, can be generalized to any IMAP-compatible service.

Setting Up the IMAP Connection

Before you start reading emails, you need to establish a connection to the mail server. If you're using Gmail, the IMAP server address is `imap.gmail.com`, and the port for IMAP over SSL is **993**.

Let's begin by setting up the connection:

```
import imaplib
```

```
# Your email credentials
email_user = "your_email@gmail.com"
email_password = "your_email_password"

# Connect to the Gmail IMAP server
mail = imaplib.IMAP4_SSL('imap.gmail.com')

# Log in to your account
mail.login(email_user, email_password)
```

In this code:

- **IMAP4_SSL()** is used to establish a secure connection with Gmail's IMAP server over SSL.
- **login()** authenticates you with your email account, using your email address and password.

Selecting the Mailbox

Once you've logged in, you need to specify which mailbox you want to access. Most email services, including Gmail, use mailboxes like "INBOX," "Sent," and "Trash." By default, we'll access the inbox to read incoming emails.

```
# Select the mailbox you want to read from
mail.select("inbox")
```

This line of code sets the **"INBOX"** as the mailbox for email retrieval. If you wanted to access a different folder (like "Sent"), you would specify that folder instead.

Searching for Emails

Now that you're connected to the inbox, the next step is to search for specific emails. IMAP lets you search for messages based on various criteria, like the sender, subject, date, or whether they've been read. You can use search criteria to filter emails that you want to process.

For example, to search for all emails that are still unread, you can use the **SEARCH** command with the keyword **"UNSEEN"**.

```
# Search for all unread emails
```

```
status, email_ids = mail.search(None, 'UNSEEN')

# Convert the result to a list of email IDs
email_ids = email_ids[0].split()
```

Here:

- **search()** is used to find emails based on the provided search criteria. We use None as the first argument because we aren't searching for any specific folder, and we use 'UNSEEN' to search for unread emails.
- **email_ids** is a list of email IDs that match the search criteria.

Fetching and Reading Email Content

Once you have the email IDs, you can fetch the emails and extract their content. We use the **fetch()** method to retrieve emails, which gives you the email's raw data. From this raw data, we can parse out the email's subject, sender, and body.

Here's how you fetch and extract details from the first unread email:

```python
# Fetch the first email using its ID
status, email_data = mail.fetch(email_ids[0], '(RFC822)')

# email_data contains raw email data; we need to parse it
for response_part in email_data:
    if isinstance(response_part, tuple):
        # Parse the email
        msg = email.message_from_bytes(response_part[1])

        # Get the email details
        subject = msg['subject']
        from_ = msg['from']
        print(f"Subject: {subject}")
        print(f"From: {from_}")

        # Get the body of the email
        if msg.is_multipart():
            for part in msg.walk():
                if part.get_content_type() == 'text/plain':
                    body =
part.get_payload(decode=True).decode()
                    print(f"Body: {body}")
        else:
            body = msg.get_payload(decode=True).decode()
            print(f"Body: {body}")
```

80

Explanation:

- **fetch()** retrieves the raw email data for the specified email ID.
- **email.message_from_bytes()** parses the raw email content into a usable format.
- We extract the **subject** and **from** fields using msg['subject'] and msg['from'].
- If the email is multipart (i.e., it contains both plain text and HTML), we loop through each part to find the **text/plain** content and extract the body.
- For non-multipart emails, we simply get the body with get_payload().

Closing the Connection

After reading the emails you need, it's important to close the connection to the server properly.

```
# Close the connection and logout
mail.close()
mail.logout()
```

This ensures that the session is ended cleanly, and any resources are freed.

Handling Errors and Debugging

Like with any network-based interaction, there are chances that something might go wrong—whether it's a network issue, incorrect credentials, or some other problem. Handling errors gracefully is essential.

Here's how you can handle errors while reading emails:

```
try:
    # Connect, login, and fetch emails as shown above
    # If everything works, the email is read successfully
    print("Email fetched successfully!")

except imaplib.IMAP4.error as e:
    print(f"IMAP error: {e}")

except Exception as e:
    print(f"Error: {e}")

finally:
```

```
# Ensure that the session is closed
mail.logout()
```

The `try-except` block captures any issues that arise, whether they're related to IMAP or something else, and prints an appropriate message.

Conclusion

Using `imaplib` to read emails in Python can significantly streamline tasks that involve monitoring and interacting with emails. Whether you're building an email-based notification system, automatically processing incoming emails, or just want to automate your inbox, `imaplib` gives you the tools you need to efficiently retrieve and parse email messages.

4.3 Using Email Templates and Attachments

When automating email communication, it's essential to make your messages look professional, personalized, and efficient. This is where **email templates** and **attachments** come in handy. Using templates ensures that your emails are consistent, while attachments allow you to share files seamlessly. In this section, we'll walk through how to create and use email templates, as well as how to send attachments with Python using the **smtplib** and **email** libraries.

Why Use Email Templates?

Email templates provide a convenient way to standardize communication, especially when you need to send out similar messages to different recipients. Whether it's a daily status update, a promotional offer, or a welcome email, templates save you time and help maintain a consistent tone and structure.

Python makes it easy to automate email content using templates. You can store these templates as plain text files, HTML files, or even use Python's built-in formatting features to inject dynamic content into the emails.

Creating Email Templates in Python

Let's first explore how to use basic string formatting to create a simple email template. This can be particularly useful for sending personalized emails to multiple recipients.

Suppose you want to send a personalized welcome email to new users. You can create a template like this:

```python
def create_welcome_email(name, username):
    subject = "Welcome to Our Service!"
    body = f"""
    Hi {name},

    Thank you for signing up for our service. Your username
is: {username}.
    We are excited to have you on board.

    Best regards,
    The Team
    """
    return subject, body
```

In this function:

- The email body is personalized using **string formatting** (`f""`), where placeholders like `{name}` and `{username}` are replaced with actual values.
- This allows you to create a dynamic message without manually editing the content for each recipient.

You can call the `create_welcome_email()` function to generate the subject and body of the email and send it out using **smtplib**.

Sending HTML Email Templates

Sometimes, you might need a more sophisticated design for your emails, especially for marketing or newsletters. HTML provides the flexibility to include styled text, images, links, and more. Here's how to send an HTML email template using Python.

```python
from email.mime.multipart import MIMEMultipart
from email.mime.text import MIMEText
```

```python
def create_html_email(name, username):
    subject = "Welcome to Our Service!"
    body = f"""
    <html>
    <body>
        <h1>Hi {name},</h1>
        <p>Thank you for signing up for our service. Your
username is: <strong>{username}</strong>.</p>
        <p>We are excited to have you on board!</p>
        <p>Best regards, <br> The Team</p>
    </body>
    </html>
    """
    return subject, body

# Send email using smtplib and MIMEText
from smtplib import SMTP

def send_email(subject, body, to_email):
    msg = MIMEMultipart()
    msg['From'] = 'your_email@gmail.com'
    msg['To'] = to_email
    msg['Subject'] = subject

    msg.attach(MIMEText(body, 'html'))

    with SMTP('smtp.gmail.com', 587) as server:
        server.starttls()  # Secure the connection
        server.login('your_email@gmail.com', 'your_password')
        server.sendmail(msg['From'], msg['To'],
msg.as_string())

# Generate the email content
subject, body = create_html_email("John Doe", "john_doe123")

# Send the email
send_email(subject, body, 'recipient@example.com')
```

In this example:

- We use the `MIMEText` class from the **email.mime.text** module to handle HTML content.
- The email body is wrapped in HTML tags, allowing you to include bold, headings, and other styles.
- The `MIMEMultipart` class is used to handle multiple parts (i.e., HTML and plain text). This is useful when sending both an HTML version and a plain text version of the email.

Sending Attachments

Email attachments are a common requirement, whether you're sending documents, images, or reports. The **email.mime** library helps you easily handle attachments by creating a MIME part for the file.

Here's how to send an email with an attachment, such as a PDF or image:

```python
from email.mime.base import MIMEBase
from email import encoders

def send_email_with_attachment(subject, body, to_email,
attachment_path):
    msg = MIMEMultipart()
    msg['From'] = 'your_email@gmail.com'
    msg['To'] = to_email
    msg['Subject'] = subject

    msg.attach(MIMEText(body, 'plain'))

    # Attach a file
    with open(attachment_path, 'rb') as attachment:
        part = MIMEBase('application', 'octet-stream')
        part.set_payload(attachment.read())
        encoders.encode_base64(part)
        part.add_header('Content-Disposition', f'attachment;
filename="{attachment_path.split("/")[-1]}"')
        msg.attach(part)

    with SMTP('smtp.gmail.com', 587) as server:
        server.starttls()  # Secure the connection
        server.login('your_email@gmail.com', 'your_password')
        server.sendmail(msg['From'], msg['To'],
msg.as_string())

# Example usage:
subject = "Monthly Report"
body = "Please find the attached monthly report."
attachment_path = "report.pdf"
send_email_with_attachment(subject, body,
'recipient@example.com', attachment_path)
```

In this code:

- The **MIMEBase** class is used to handle the attachment.
- **encoders.encode_base64(part)** is necessary to encode the attachment so it can be safely transmitted over email.

- The `Content-Disposition` header specifies that the attachment is a file to be downloaded by the recipient.

Conclusion

Using email templates and attachments in your Python email automation scripts can significantly enhance the professionalism and functionality of your messages. Templates help maintain consistency and personalization, while attachments enable you to share files directly with recipients.

This flexibility is essential when automating tasks like daily reports, sending invoices, or distributing newsletters. By combining these features with the power of Python, you can automate email workflows that would otherwise be time-consuming and repetitive.

4.4 Messaging with WhatsApp/Telegram APIs

In this section, we will explore how to automate messaging using two popular platforms: **WhatsApp** and **Telegram**. These messaging services have robust APIs (Application Programming Interfaces) that allow developers to send messages programmatically, making them perfect for automating notifications, alerts, or any messaging task.

While both platforms offer messaging APIs, they have slightly different approaches to usage, authentication, and functionality. In this guide, we'll cover both WhatsApp and Telegram messaging automation.

Automating Messages with the WhatsApp API

WhatsApp's official API is part of the **WhatsApp Business API**, which is designed for medium to large businesses. However, for personal and smaller-scale projects, there are libraries such as `pywhatkit` and `whatsapp-web` that allow sending WhatsApp messages without needing access to the official API.

To get started with `pywhatkit`, which is an easy-to-use library, follow the steps below:

1. **Install pywhatkit**: To use the library, install it via pip:

```
pip install pywhatkit
```

2. **Sending a WhatsApp Message**: The most basic feature of pywhatkit is sending a WhatsApp message at a specific time. Here's how you can send a message:

```
import pywhatkit as kit

# Send a WhatsApp message
kit.sendwhatmsg("+1234567890", "Hello, this is an
automated message!", 15, 30)
```

Explanation:

- o "+1234567890": The recipient's phone number, including the country code.
- o "Hello, this is an automated message!": The message content.
- o 15, 30: The time when the message should be sent (in hours and minutes, in 24-hour format).

When this code is run, WhatsApp will open on your computer and automatically send the message at the specified time.

3. **Sending WhatsApp Messages with Media**: If you want to send an image or other media, pywhatkit also provides that functionality:

```
kit.sendwhats_image("+1234567890", "path_to_image.jpg",
"Automated image message!")
```

This will send an image file located at the specified path with an optional caption.

4. **Limitations**: While pywhatkit is convenient for personal use, keep in mind that this method relies on web.whatsapp.com being logged in and requires a live connection. For larger-scale automation or businesses, you'll want to explore the WhatsApp Business API, which requires a verified phone number and is designed for integrating with customer service platforms.

Automating Messages with the Telegram API

Telegram, on the other hand, offers a more straightforward and open API for developers, allowing both personal and large-scale bots to send messages. Telegram's Bot API enables you to create bots that can interact with users and automate communication.

Here's how to get started with the Telegram Bot API:

1. **Create a Telegram Bot**:
   o First, you need to create a bot on Telegram. To do this, open the Telegram app, search for **BotFather**, and follow the instructions to create a new bot. BotFather will give you an API token, which is crucial for interacting with the Telegram API.
2. **Install Python Libraries**: The most popular library for working with the Telegram API in Python is `python-telegram-bot`. You can install it via pip:

```
pip install python-telegram-bot
```

3. **Sending a Message with the Telegram Bot API**: With the API token you received from BotFather, you can now send messages. Here's a simple example of how to send a message:

```
from telegram import Bot

# Initialize the bot with your token
bot = Bot(token='YOUR_BOT_API_TOKEN')

# Send a message to a specific chat
chat_id = '@your_channel_or_chat_id'  # You can use a
username or chat ID
bot.send_message(chat_id=chat_id, text="Hello, this is
an automated message from my bot!")
```

Explanation:

   o `YOUR_BOT_API_TOKEN`: Replace this with the API token you got from BotFather.
   o `chat_id`: This can be either a specific user's chat ID or a group/channel's username (e.g., `@your_channel`).
   o `text`: The content of the message.

4. **Handling Multiple Messages**: You can also send multiple messages, respond to messages from users, and automate notifications based on certain events. Here's an example of how you could create a bot that automatically replies to messages:

```python
from telegram.ext import Updater, CommandHandler

def start(update, context):
    update.message.reply_text("Hello, welcome to the bot!")

updater = Updater('YOUR_BOT_API_TOKEN', use_context=True)
dispatcher = updater.dispatcher

# Register the /start command
dispatcher.add_handler(CommandHandler('start', start))

updater.start_polling()
updater.idle()
```

This bot listens for the `/start` command and replies with a greeting.

5. **Sending Messages with Media**: Similar to WhatsApp, Telegram allows you to send media such as photos and videos. Here's an example of how to send an image with your bot:

```python
bot.send_photo(chat_id=chat_id, photo=open('path_to_image.jpg', 'rb'))
```

In this case, the bot will send an image located at `path_to_image.jpg`.

Which Platform to Choose?

- **WhatsApp**: If your primary audience uses WhatsApp, or you want to automate communication on a personal scale, WhatsApp's Business API or the `pywhatkit` library will work well for small-scale use cases.
- **Telegram**: For larger-scale projects or when you need a more flexible, open API that allows for sophisticated automation (like chatbots, group notifications, etc.), Telegram is a great choice. Its

ease of use and rich features make it suitable for both personal and business applications.

Conclusion

Both **WhatsApp** and **Telegram** provide powerful APIs for automating messaging. While WhatsApp is a popular platform for personal communication and is often used for customer engagement, Telegram offers more developer-friendly APIs for creating sophisticated bots and automating tasks.

With the right Python libraries, you can easily set up bots to send messages, handle media, and integrate with other services to streamline your communication processes. Whether for personal productivity or large-scale business automation, both platforms can significantly enhance your workflow.

4.5 Project: Automated Daily Email Reporter

In this section, we'll build a project that automates sending daily email reports. Imagine you're working in an environment where you need to send out daily updates to a group of colleagues or clients, whether it's for work progress, sales data, or website analytics. Automating this process saves time and ensures that your reports are sent out consistently.

The main goal of this project is to build a Python script that gathers data, formats it, and sends it out as an email at a specified time each day. By the end of this guide, you'll have a fully functioning automated email reporting system.

Step 1: Setting Up the Environment

Before diving into the code, make sure you have the following Python libraries installed:

- **smtplib**: This is Python's built-in library for sending emails.

- **email.mime**: Used to create MIME (Multipurpose Internet Mail Extensions) objects, which are necessary for structuring email content (such as plain text, HTML, or attachments).
- **schedule**: This library is used for scheduling tasks, so we can automate the process of sending the email at specific times.

Install the necessary libraries via pip (if you don't have `schedule` installed yet):

```
pip install schedule
```

Step 2: Writing the Email Sender Function

The first part of the project is writing a function that can send an email. We'll use Python's built-in **smtplib** for this.

Here's a basic version of the function to send an email:

```
import smtplib
from email.mime.text import MIMEText
from email.mime.multipart import MIMEMultipart

def send_email(subject, body, to_email):
    from_email = "your_email@example.com"  # Your email
    password = "your_email_password"  # Your email password
or app-specific password

    # Set up the MIME
    msg = MIMEMultipart()
    msg['From'] = from_email
    msg['To'] = to_email
    msg['Subject'] = subject

    # Attach the email body
    msg.attach(MIMEText(body, 'plain'))

    # Set up the server and send the email
    try:
        server = smtplib.SMTP('smtp.gmail.com', 587)  # For
Gmail
        server.starttls()  # Secure the connection
        server.login(from_email, password)  # Log in to the
email account
        text = msg.as_string()
        server.sendmail(from_email, to_email, text)  # Send
email
```

```
        server.quit()   # Close the server connection
        print("Email sent successfully!")
    except Exception as e:
        print(f"Failed to send email. Error: {e}")
```

- **Explanation**:
  - o We are using `smtplib.SMTP` to connect to the email server (Gmail in this case).
  - o `MIMEMultipart` and `MIMEText` help create the structure of the email, allowing us to add both the subject and body, which can be plain text or HTML.
  - o The server is authenticated via `server.login()`, where you'll need your email address and either your password or an app-specific password if using Gmail.

Step 3: Scheduling the Email Report

Now that we have the basic email function, let's focus on automating the sending of the email. We'll use the `schedule` library to make this process run automatically at a specified time every day.

```
import schedule
import time

def daily_report():
    subject = "Daily Sales Report"
    body = "Here is your daily sales update: \n\nTotal Sales:
$500\nOrders Completed: 150"
    to_email = "recipient_email@example.com"
    send_email(subject, body, to_email)

# Schedule the email to be sent at 9:00 AM every day
schedule.every().day.at("09:00").do(daily_report)

# Keep the script running to execute the scheduled tasks
while True:
    schedule.run_pending()
    time.sleep(60)   # Check for scheduled tasks every minute
```

- **Explanation**:
  - o The `daily_report()` function is where you define the content of your daily email. You can customize the body with dynamic data (e.g., from a file, database, or API).

- o Using
  `schedule.every().day.at("09:00").do(daily_report)`,
  we set the email to be sent every day at 9:00 AM.
- o The `while True` loop ensures the script continuously checks
  and runs the scheduled tasks, sending the email daily.

Step 4: Adding Dynamic Content

Instead of sending static content (like the example in the `body`), you might
want to send reports that change daily. For this, you can generate dynamic
content by querying a database, reading a CSV file, or calling an API.

For example, let's imagine you want to pull sales data from a CSV file to
include in the email:

```
import csv

def generate_report():
    total_sales = 0
    total_orders = 0

    # Read data from a CSV file
    with open('sales_data.csv', mode='r') as file:
        csv_reader = csv.reader(file)
        for row in csv_reader:
            total_sales += float(row[1])  # Assuming sales
data is in the second column
            total_orders += int(row[2])   # Assuming order
count is in the third column

    return f"Total Sales: ${total_sales}\nOrders Completed:
{total_orders}"

def daily_report():
    subject = "Daily Sales Report"
    body = f"Here is your daily sales
update:\n\n{generate_report()}"
    to_email = "recipient_email@example.com"
    send_email(subject, body, to_email)
```

Here, the `generate_report()` function reads sales data from a CSV file and
calculates the total sales and number of orders. This dynamically generated
report is then included in the email body.

Step 5: Running the Script

Once you have written the script, simply run it on a server or your local machine, and it will automatically send emails at the scheduled time every day. To ensure it runs continuously, you might consider setting up the script on a server that's always on, or use task schedulers like **cron** (Linux/Mac) or **Task Scheduler** (Windows) to execute the script at the same time every day.

Conclusion

Congratulations! You've just built an automated daily email reporter using Python. In this project, you learned how to send emails using Python, automate the process with a scheduling library, and generate dynamic email content.

This basic framework can be adapted for many different scenarios, whether you're sending daily reports, reminders, or notifications. As you gain more experience, you can explore adding more sophisticated content, such as sending attachments, integrating with external data sources, or even creating HTML-formatted emails for better presentation.

Chapter 5: Working with Excel, CSV, and PDF

Spreadsheets and PDFs are everywhere—used in offices, schools, finance departments, and even by individuals managing their own budgets. In this chapter, we're going to learn how to automate common tasks involving CSV, Excel, and PDF files using Python. Whether you're managing an inventory list, analyzing monthly expenses, or sending out batch reports, this chapter will arm you with the tools to do it faster and more reliably.

Why Automate These File Types?

Manually editing CSVs and spreadsheets or copying and merging PDFs might seem harmless for small tasks, but it becomes a serious time sink at scale. Python offers clean and consistent APIs to handle all of these files. You can read data, generate reports, update spreadsheets, and even modify PDFs—all with just a few lines of code.

Let's walk through each format and the key tasks you can automate.

5.1 Reading and Writing CSV Files

CSV files—Comma Separated Values—are one of the most common formats for storing structured data. They're used in everything from exporting contacts and sales records to logging server data. Fortunately, Python comes with a built-in module called `csv` that makes working with these files incredibly straightforward.

Let's dive into how you can read and write CSV files effectively, with real-world examples and practical tips to make your scripts robust and maintainable.

Why Use CSV?

CSV files are lightweight, human-readable, and supported by almost every data-processing application, including Excel, Google Sheets, and database importers. Their simplicity is both their strength and limitation—there's no formatting, formulas, or styling, just raw data. But that's exactly what makes them ideal for automation.

Reading CSV Files in Python

Suppose you have a `sales.csv` file like this:

```
Date,Product,Amount
2024-04-01,Laptop,1200
2024-04-01,Mouse,25
2024-04-02,Keyboard,75
```

To read this file:

```python
import csv

with open('sales.csv', mode='r', newline='') as file:
    reader = csv.reader(file)
    for row in reader:
        print(row)
```

What's happening here:

- `csv.reader(file)` creates an iterator over rows.
- Each `row` is returned as a list of strings.
- `newline=''` ensures correct handling of line endings across platforms.

To make your code more readable and powerful, consider using `csv.DictReader`, which returns each row as a dictionary using the headers:

```python
with open('sales.csv', mode='r', newline='') as file:
    reader = csv.DictReader(file)
    for row in reader:
        print(f"{row['Date']} - {row['Product']}:
${row['Amount']}")
```

This approach is ideal when the structure of the CSV is consistent and headers are present.

Writing CSV Files

Let's say you want to log a new set of sales data. You can use `csv.writer` to create a CSV file:

```python
import csv

data = [
    ['Date', 'Product', 'Amount'],
    ['2024-04-03', 'Monitor', 300],
    ['2024-04-03', 'HDMI Cable', 15]
]

with open('new_sales.csv', mode='w', newline='') as file:
    writer = csv.writer(file)
    writer.writerows(data)
```

Note:

- `writerows()` writes multiple rows at once.
- Always include `newline=''` to avoid extra blank lines, especially on Windows.

If you want to write rows as dictionaries, use `csv.DictWriter`:

```python
data = [
    {'Date': '2024-04-04', 'Product': 'Tablet', 'Amount': 550},
    {'Date': '2024-04-04', 'Product': 'Stylus', 'Amount': 35}
]

with open('dict_sales.csv', mode='w', newline='') as file:
    fieldnames = ['Date', 'Product', 'Amount']
    writer = csv.DictWriter(file, fieldnames=fieldnames)
    writer.writeheader()
    writer.writerows(data)
```

This makes your code more flexible and easier to scale—especially when working with APIs or other dictionary-based data sources.

97

Appending to Existing Files

Automation often involves *adding* data rather than replacing it. To append rows:

```
new_entries = [
    ['2024-04-05', 'Webcam', 85],
    ['2024-04-05', 'Microphone', 120]
]

with open('sales.csv', mode='a', newline='') as file:
    writer = csv.writer(file)
    writer.writerows(new_entries)
```

Using `'a'` mode ensures you don't overwrite existing data—great for loggers and periodic trackers.

Practical Tips and Gotchas

- **Always handle encoding** if working with international characters. Use `encoding='utf-8'` or `encoding='utf-8-sig'` as needed.
- **Validate your data** before writing—incorrect rows can corrupt the CSV format.
- **Use try-except blocks** for better error handling, especially when working with external CSVs.
- **Avoid Excel-specific quirks** by sticking to standard CSV formatting (no formulas, embedded commas, or line breaks in fields unless properly quoted).

Example: Sales Summarizer Script

Here's a script that reads a CSV, calculates total sales, and writes the summary to a new file.

```
import csv
from collections import defaultdict

totals = defaultdict(float)

with open('sales.csv', mode='r', newline='') as file:
```

```
reader = csv.DictReader(file)
for row in reader:
    product = row['Product']
    amount = float(row['Amount'])
    totals[product] += amount

with open('sales_summary.csv', mode='w', newline='') as file:
    writer = csv.writer(file)
    writer.writerow(['Product', 'Total Amount'])
    for product, total in totals.items():
        writer.writerow([product, round(total, 2)])
```

This is the kind of automation that would take minutes manually and just seconds with a script—plus it's reproducible.

When to Use CSVs vs Excel

- Use **CSV** for simple, flat data and interoperability.
- Use **Excel** when you need formatting, formulas, or charts (which we'll cover in the next section).

Wrap-Up

CSV automation is one of the most impactful Python skills you can learn. Whether you're parsing logs, generating reports, or feeding data into other tools, Python's csv module makes it painless. Once you're comfortable with CSVs, you'll find many automation tasks suddenly feel within reach.

5.2 Automating Excel with openpyxl

Excel remains a staple in data management across various industries. While manual operations suffice for small datasets, automation becomes essential when dealing with large volumes of data or repetitive tasks. Python's openpyxl library offers a robust solution for automating Excel tasks, enabling you to read, write, and modify .xlsx files efficiently.

Getting Started with openpyxl

To begin, ensure that `openpyxl` is installed in your Python environment:

```
pip install openpyxl
```

Once installed, you can start creating and manipulating Excel workbooks.

Creating a New Workbook

Creating a new Excel workbook is straightforward:

```python
from openpyxl import Workbook

# Create a new workbook
wb = Workbook()

# Access the active worksheet
ws = wb.active
ws.title = "SalesData"

# Add data to the worksheet
ws.append(["Date", "Product", "Revenue"])
ws.append(["2025-04-01", "Laptop", 1200])
ws.append(["2025-04-02", "Smartphone", 800])

# Save the workbook
wb.save("sales_data.xlsx")
```

This script initializes a new workbook, sets the title of the active worksheet, appends rows of data, and saves the file as `sales_data.xlsx`.

Reading and Modifying Existing Workbooks

To read and modify an existing Excel file:

```python
from openpyxl import load_workbook

# Load an existing workbook
wb = load_workbook("sales_data.xlsx")

# Select the desired worksheet
```

```
ws = wb["SalesData"]

# Read data from a specific cell
product = ws["B2"].value
print(f"Product in B2: {product}")

# Modify the value of a cell
ws["C2"] = 1300   # Update revenue

# Save the changes
wb.save("sales_data_updated.xlsx")
```

This code loads the existing `sales_data.xlsx` file, accesses the "SalesData" worksheet, reads the value from cell B2, updates the revenue in cell C2, and saves the changes to a new file.

Applying Styles and Formatting

Enhancing the visual appeal of your Excel files can be achieved by applying styles:

```
from openpyxl.styles import Font, PatternFill

# Apply bold font to header row
for cell in ws[1]:
    cell.font = Font(bold=True)

# Apply a fill color to the header row
fill = PatternFill(start_color="FFFF00", end_color="FFFF00",
fill_type="solid")
for cell in ws[1]:
    cell.fill = fill

# Save the styled workbook
wb.save("sales_data_styled.xlsx")
```

This script applies bold formatting and a yellow fill to the header row, enhancing readability.

Creating Charts

Visualizing data through charts can provide valuable insights:

```
from openpyxl.chart import BarChart, Reference

# Create a bar chart
chart = BarChart()
chart.title = "Revenue by Product"
chart.x_axis.title = "Product"
chart.y_axis.title = "Revenue"

# Define data for the chart
data = Reference(ws, min_col=3, min_row=1, max_row=3)
categories = Reference(ws, min_col=2, min_row=2, max_row=3)
chart.add_data(data, titles_from_data=True)
chart.set_categories(categories)

# Add the chart to the worksheet
ws.add_chart(chart, "E5")

# Save the workbook with the chart
wb.save("sales_data_chart.xlsx")
```

This code creates a bar chart titled "Revenue by Product," using the data from the worksheet, and inserts it into cell E5.

Best Practices and Tips

- **Data Validation**: Ensure that the data types are consistent, especially when performing calculations or generating charts.
- **Error Handling**: Implement try-except blocks to handle potential errors, such as missing files or incorrect worksheet names.
- **Efficient Iteration**: Use `ws.iter_rows()` or `ws.iter_cols()` for efficient iteration over large datasets. (A Guide to Excel Spreadsheets in Python With openpyxl)
- **Resource Management**: Always close workbooks after operations to free up system resources.

Conclusion

Automating Excel tasks with `openpyxl` can significantly enhance productivity, especially when dealing with repetitive tasks or large datasets. By leveraging Python's capabilities, you can create, modify, and analyze

Excel files programmatically, leading to more efficient workflows and reduced manual errors.

As you continue to explore `openpyxl`, you'll discover more advanced features, such as conditional formatting, data validation, and working with formulas, further expanding your ability to automate complex Excel tasks.

5.3 Generating Reports and Charts

In many workplaces, generating reports is part of the daily grind—pulling numbers, organizing data, formatting spreadsheets, and creating visualizations. It's a task that can be tedious and time-consuming if done manually. Luckily, Python makes it surprisingly easy to automate this entire process. With a few libraries like `openpyxl`, `matplotlib`, and `pandas`, you can produce polished, dynamic reports and charts with minimal effort.

Getting Started

Let's imagine a scenario: You receive daily or weekly sales data in CSV format, and your job is to generate a summary report with both tabular data and charts. We'll walk through automating that—from reading the data, summarizing it, generating an Excel report, and embedding charts.

First, install the necessary libraries if you haven't already:

```
pip install pandas openpyxl matplotlib
```

Reading the Data

Assume you have a CSV file like `sales_data.csv`:

```
Date,Product,Units Sold,Unit Price
2025-04-01,Laptop,4,1200
2025-04-01,Smartphone,6,800
2025-04-02,Laptop,3,1200
2025-04-02,Smartphone,5,800
```

Now, read it using pandas and compute total revenue per product:

```
import pandas as pd
```

```
# Load sales data
df = pd.read_csv("sales_data.csv")

# Calculate revenue
df["Revenue"] = df["Units Sold"] * df["Unit Price"]

# Summarize revenue by product
summary =
df.groupby("Product")["Revenue"].sum().reset_index()
summary
```

At this point, the `summary` DataFrame gives you the total revenue per product.

Writing to Excel with openpyxl

Now let's write both the detailed data and the summary into an Excel file:

```
with pd.ExcelWriter("sales_report.xlsx", engine="openpyxl")
as writer:
    df.to_excel(writer, sheet_name="Detailed Data",
index=False)
    summary.to_excel(writer, sheet_name="Summary",
index=False)
```

This creates a neat Excel file with two sheets: one for the detailed sales data and another for the summary.

Generating Charts with matplotlib

Next, let's create a bar chart showing revenue per product. While `matplotlib` isn't required for Excel charts (since `openpyxl` supports basic charts), it's great for generating image-based charts to include in reports or send in emails.

```
import matplotlib.pyplot as plt

# Create a bar chart
plt.figure(figsize=(8, 5))
plt.bar(summary["Product"], summary["Revenue"],
color="skyblue")
plt.title("Total Revenue by Product")
plt.xlabel("Product")
plt.ylabel("Revenue ($)")
plt.tight_layout()
```

```
# Save the chart
plt.savefig("revenue_chart.png")
plt.close()
```

This generates and saves the chart as `revenue_chart.png`.

Inserting the Chart into Excel

While `matplotlib` is great for images, if you prefer Excel-native charts, `openpyxl` lets you add them too. Let's see how to insert a bar chart into the Excel report:

```
from openpyxl import load_workbook
from openpyxl.chart import BarChart, Reference

# Load the existing workbook
wb = load_workbook("sales_report.xlsx")
ws = wb["Summary"]

# Define the data and categories
data = Reference(ws, min_col=2, min_row=1,
max_row=ws.max_row)
categories = Reference(ws, min_col=1, min_row=2,
max_row=ws.max_row)

# Create and configure the chart
chart = BarChart()
chart.title = "Total Revenue by Product"
chart.x_axis.title = "Product"
chart.y_axis.title = "Revenue"
chart.add_data(data, titles_from_data=True)
chart.set_categories(categories)

# Add the chart to the worksheet
ws.add_chart(chart, "D2")

# Save the updated file
wb.save("sales_report_with_chart.xlsx")
```

This places a dynamic bar chart directly into your Excel workbook, making it ready for presentation or sharing.

Bringing It All Together

By combining these tools, you can easily automate:

- Data ingestion from CSV or databases
- Data aggregation and transformation using pandas
- Report creation with openpyxl
- Chart generation using either openpyxl or matplotlib

This entire workflow can be encapsulated in a single script and scheduled to run daily, weekly, or on demand—saving hours of manual work.

Final Thoughts

Once you get comfortable with this approach, it opens the door to all kinds of automation possibilities: monthly performance dashboards, client reporting, budget tracking—you name it. And the best part? Once your script is set up, your reports will generate themselves while you grab a coffee.

5.4 Reading and Merging PDFs with PyPDF2

PDFs are everywhere—from invoices to reports and manuals. If you've ever had to combine multiple PDFs into one file or extract specific pages from a large document, you know how repetitive that can get. Python offers a powerful way to automate these tasks using the `PyPDF2` library.

Let's walk through how to use `PyPDF2` to read, extract, and merge PDFs with clarity and efficiency.

Getting Started with PyPDF2

Start by installing the library (if you haven't already):

```
pip install PyPDF2
```

Once installed, you're ready to automate some of the most common PDF operations.

Reading and Extracting Text from a PDF

Let's say you have a PDF called `sample.pdf`, and you want to extract all the text from the first page.

```
from PyPDF2 import PdfReader

reader = PdfReader("sample.pdf")
first_page = reader.pages[0]
text = first_page.extract_text()

print(text)
```

This simple script opens the PDF, grabs the first page, and extracts its text content. It works well on text-based PDFs (not scanned images).

If you want to extract from *all* pages, loop through them:

```
for page in reader.pages:
    print(page.extract_text())
```

This is useful when you want to build searchable archives or extract data from forms or receipts.

Merging Multiple PDF Files

Combining PDFs is another highly useful task, especially when dealing with scanned reports or invoices saved as separate files.

Here's how you can merge multiple PDFs into one:

```
from PyPDF2 import PdfMerger

merger = PdfMerger()

files_to_merge = ["report_part1.pdf", "report_part2.pdf",
"appendix.pdf"]

for pdf in files_to_merge:
    merger.append(pdf)

merger.write("combined_report.pdf")
merger.close()
```

This script merges the PDFs in the order they're listed and writes out a single file named `combined_report.pdf`.

Tip: Always double-check the order of files when merging—it's easy to mix them up when dealing with large batches.

Extracting Specific Pages

What if you only need pages 2–4 from a 10-page document?

```python
from PyPDF2 import PdfWriter

reader = PdfReader("long_report.pdf")
writer = PdfWriter()

for page_num in range(1, 4):  # Page numbers are zero-based
    writer.add_page(reader.pages[page_num])

with open("excerpt.pdf", "wb") as f:
    writer.write(f)
```

This is perfect for isolating chapters, relevant reports, or summaries without editing the document manually.

Rotating or Reordering Pages

You can even rotate pages, which is useful if scanned pages come in upside-down:

```python
from PyPDF2 import PdfReader, PdfWriter

reader = PdfReader("scan.pdf")
writer = PdfWriter()

rotated_page = reader.pages[0].rotate(90)  # Rotate 90
degrees clockwise
writer.add_page(rotated_page)

with open("rotated_scan.pdf", "wb") as f:
    writer.write(f)
```

Reordering is just a matter of changing the order in which you add pages to `PdfWriter`.

Limitations of PyPDF2

While PyPDF2 is excellent for basic tasks, it doesn't support:

- Editing PDF content (text/images)
- Extracting text from image-based (scanned) PDFs
- Adding annotations or bookmarks
- Handling complex layouts with rich formatting

If you need more advanced capabilities, libraries like `pdfplumber`, `PDFMiner`, or `pypdfium2` are worth exploring. But for most automation involving extraction and merging, `PyPDF2` gets the job done.

Automating a Real-World Workflow

Let's say you receive a weekly batch of reports from different teams—each in its own PDF—and you want to:

- Combine them into a single document
- Extract a one-page executive summary
- Save both files automatically

Here's a complete automation script:

```python
from PyPDF2 import PdfReader, PdfWriter, PdfMerger

# Step 1: Merge PDFs
report_files = ["teamA.pdf", "teamB.pdf", "teamC.pdf"]
merger = PdfMerger()

for file in report_files:
    merger.append(file)

merger.write("full_weekly_report.pdf")
merger.close()
```

```
# Step 2: Extract summary page (assume page 0 of teamA is the
summary)
reader = PdfReader("teamA.pdf")
writer = PdfWriter()
writer.add_page(reader.pages[0])

with open("executive_summary.pdf", "wb") as f:
    writer.write(f)
```

You can run this script each week to automate a task that might otherwise take 10–15 minutes manually.

Final Thoughts

Whether you're managing student records, compiling legal documents, or generating financial summaries, automating your PDF workflows can be a major time-saver. While `PyPDF2` isn't perfect, its simplicity makes it ideal for beginners looking to level up their productivity with Python.

5.5 Project: Automated Expense Tracker

Keeping track of expenses is one of those essential but often neglected habits. Most of us start the month with the best intentions, maybe even a spreadsheet template, and then... forget to update it after week one. That's where automation shines. In this project, you'll build a Python-based expense tracker that pulls data from CSV or Excel files, categorizes expenses, and generates a summary report—automatically.

The tools we'll use:

- `csv` or `openpyxl` to read the data.
- `collections` and simple logic for categorization.
- `matplotlib` for visualizing where the money goes.
- Optional PDF reporting with `reportlab` or `PyPDF2` (if you'd like to go further).

Let's break it down step by step.

Step 1: Prepare the Expense Data

Assume you export a CSV file from your bank app that looks like this:

```
Date,Description,Amount,Type
2025-04-01,Coffee Shop,-4.50,Debit
2025-04-02,Salary,2000.00,Credit
2025-04-03,Groceries,-72.00,Debit
```

Save this file as `expenses.csv`. We'll parse and process this file first.

```python
import csv
from collections import defaultdict

def read_expenses(file_path):
    expenses = []
    with open(file_path, newline='', encoding='utf-8') as f:
        reader = csv.DictReader(f)
        for row in reader:
            try:
                amount = float(row['Amount'])
                expenses.append({
                    'date': row['Date'],
                    'description': row['Description'],
                    'amount': amount,
                    'type': row['Type']
                })
            except ValueError:
                continue  # skip invalid rows
    return expenses
```

You now have a clean list of expense entries to work with.

Step 2: Categorize Transactions

To make your report meaningful, group transactions into categories (food, rent, utilities, entertainment, etc.). You could build a simple rule-based system for this.

```python
def categorize(description):
    desc = description.lower()
    if "grocery" in desc or "market" in desc:
        return "Groceries"
    elif "coffee" in desc or "restaurant" in desc:
        return "Dining"
```

```
    elif "uber" in desc or "lyft" in desc:
        return "Transport"
    elif "rent" in desc:
        return "Rent"
    elif "salary" in desc:
        return "Income"
    else:
        return "Other"
```

You can always expand these rules or load them from a config file later.

Step 3: Summarize Expenses by Category

Now that each transaction has a category, calculate how much you spent per category.

```
def summarize_expenses(expenses):
    summary = defaultdict(float)
    for entry in expenses:
        if entry['amount'] < 0:  # we only want debits here
            category = categorize(entry['description'])
            summary[category] += abs(entry['amount'])
    return dict(summary)
```

You're almost ready to report—let's visualize.

Step 4: Create a Pie Chart of Spending

A visual summary helps make the data instantly understandable.

```
import matplotlib.pyplot as plt

def plot_expenses(summary, output_path="expenses_chart.png"):
    categories = list(summary.keys())
    amounts = list(summary.values())

    plt.figure(figsize=(8, 8))
    plt.pie(amounts, labels=categories, autopct='%1.1f%%',
startangle=140)
    plt.title('Expense Breakdown by Category')
    plt.tight_layout()
    plt.savefig(output_path)
    plt.close()
```

This generates a pie chart and saves it as an image. You can embed this in a report, attach it to an email, or display it in a dashboard.

Step 5: Generate a Summary Report (Optional PDF)

If you want a polished PDF output for your records, you can use `reportlab`:

```
pip install reportlab
from reportlab.lib.pagesizes import A4
from reportlab.pdfgen import canvas

def generate_pdf_report(summary, chart_image,
filename="expense_report.pdf"):
    c = canvas.Canvas(filename, pagesize=A4)
    width, height = A4

    c.setFont("Helvetica-Bold", 16)
    c.drawString(50, height - 50, "Monthly Expense Report")

    c.setFont("Helvetica", 12)
    y = height - 100
    for category, amount in summary.items():
        c.drawString(50, y, f"{category}: ${amount:.2f}")
        y -= 20

    c.drawImage(chart_image, 200, y - 200, width=200,
height=200)

    c.save()
```

This report can be auto-generated and stored monthly or even emailed using scripts from the previous chapter.

Wrapping It All Up

Here's how everything ties together:

```
if __name__ == "__main__":
    data = read_expenses("expenses.csv")
    summary = summarize_expenses(data)
    plot_expenses(summary)
    generate_pdf_report(summary, "expenses_chart.png")
    print("Expense report generated successfully.")
```

Run this script every month—or even every week—to stay on top of your spending. You could also schedule it using a task scheduler like cron (Linux/macOS) or Task Scheduler (Windows).

Final Thoughts

Automating personal finance may not seem like much, but it has a tangible impact. It saves time, creates consistency, and gives you visibility into where your money goes. The more tedious the task, the more rewarding it is to automate.

Part III: Taking Automation Further

Chapter 6: Scheduling and Triggers

One of the most powerful elements of automation is timing. After all, what good is a script if you have to remember to run it manually? Whether you want to back up files daily, clean up folders weekly, or send a report every morning, you'll need to schedule and trigger your scripts automatically.

In this chapter, we'll walk through different ways to schedule Python scripts—from built-in solutions like `schedule` and `time`, to system-level tools like cron (Mac/Linux) and Task Scheduler (Windows). By the end, you'll be able to fully automate tasks on any schedule you define.

Why Scheduling Matters

Imagine building a powerful script that summarizes your expenses or backs up your work, but you forget to run it for a week. Automation isn't just about creating the tool—it's about making it *run itself*. Scheduled scripts bridge that gap. They're the invisible gears that keep your automation systems turning while you sleep.

6.1 Using Python's `schedule` and `time` Modules

When it comes to automation, timing is everything. A script that runs only when you remember to execute it isn't much of an automation tool. That's where Python's `schedule` and `time` modules come in. These libraries make it possible to run Python code at regular intervals—like every 5 minutes, once an hour, or every day at 8:00 AM—without relying on external tools.

In this section, you'll learn how to use `schedule` to define recurring jobs and how to keep your program running using the built-in `time` module.

Why Use `schedule`?

The `schedule` library abstracts away the complexity of dealing with clocks and time zones. You write what *should* happen and *when*, and it handles the rest. It's lightweight, easy to read, and a great solution for scripts that should run continuously in the background.

Let's get it installed first:

```
pip install schedule
```

A Simple Example

Let's start with a basic use case: printing a message every minute.

```python
import schedule
import time
from datetime import datetime

def task():
    now = datetime.now().strftime('%Y-%m-%d %H:%M:%S')
    print(f"Task executed at {now}")

schedule.every(1).minutes.do(task)

while True:
    schedule.run_pending()
    time.sleep(1)
```

What's happening here is straightforward:

- `schedule.every(1).minutes.do(task)` tells Python to run `task()` every minute.
- `run_pending()` checks if it's time to run any scheduled tasks.
- `time.sleep(1)` prevents the loop from hogging the CPU.

This script will keep running until you stop it manually.

Scheduling with Precision

You're not limited to "every minute" or "every hour." `schedule` lets you define times and conditions intuitively:

```
schedule.every().day.at("08:00").do(task)          # Run daily
at 8 AM
schedule.every().monday.at("09:00").do(task)       # Run every
Monday at 9 AM
schedule.every(10).seconds.do(task)                # Run every
10 seconds
schedule.every(3).hours.do(task)                   # Run every 3
hours
```

You can also chain conditions. For instance:

```
schedule.every().wednesday.at("12:00").do(task)
```

This executes only on Wednesdays at noon. You could use this for weekly summary reports, backups, or routine maintenance.

Passing Arguments to Scheduled Functions

If your task needs parameters, you can pass them using `args` or `kwargs`.

```
def greet(name):
    print(f"Hello, {name}!")

schedule.every(1).minutes.do(greet, name="Alice")
```

This flexibility allows you to reuse functions for different scheduled jobs without redefining them.

Running Multiple Jobs

You can schedule as many jobs as you need. Just define each with its own schedule:

```
schedule.every().hour.do(lambda: print("Hourly check"))
```

```
schedule.every().day.at("20:00").do(lambda: print("Daily
report at 8 PM"))
```

They'll all run within the same loop:

```
while True:
    schedule.run_pending()
    time.sleep(1)
```

Each job is tracked independently and will run at its scheduled time.

A Real-World Scenario: Website Uptime Monitor

Suppose you want to check if your website is online every 5 minutes:

```
import requests

def check_website():
    try:
        response = requests.get("https://example.com")
        if response.status_code == 200:
            print("Site is up!")
        else:
            print(f"Site returned status code
{response.status_code}")
    except Exception as e:
        print(f"Error reaching site: {e}")

schedule.every(5).minutes.do(check_website)

while True:
    schedule.run_pending()
    time.sleep(1)
```

This type of script is perfect for Raspberry Pi setups or cloud-hosted bots running 24/7.

Considerations and Limitations

While schedule is great for simple, always-on scripts, it does have some boundaries:

- It only runs when your script is running. If you shut down the machine or close the terminal, your jobs stop.
- It's best suited for light to medium workloads.
- It doesn't persist tasks after crashes or reboots—unlike cron or Task Scheduler.

If you need robustness, consider wrapping your script in a systemd service (Linux), or running it with Task Scheduler (Windows) or `nohup`.

Final Thoughts

Using `schedule` with `time` makes it easy to dip into automation without diving into system-level tools. It's an excellent fit for small-scale tasks—automated reports, file cleanups, API calls—that benefit from predictable, repeated execution.

You don't need a degree in system administration to schedule Python tasks. Sometimes, a simple `schedule.every().day.at("09:00")` is all it takes to make your day more efficient.

6.2 Setting Up Cron Jobs (Mac/Linux)

If you want your Python scripts to run without manual intervention—even when you're not logged in—**cron** is the tool for the job. Built into all Unix-like systems, including macOS and most Linux distributions, cron is a time-based job scheduler that automates tasks based on specific time and date patterns. Whether it's a daily backup, a weekly report, or a script that keeps your files organized, cron helps keep your automation running silently in the background.

Understanding Cron

Cron works using what's called a **crontab** (short for "cron table")—a simple text file that contains a list of commands and the schedule on which they should be run.

A cron entry has the following structure:

```
* * * * * /path/to/command
│ │ │ │ │
│ │ │ │ └──── Day of week (0 - 6) (Sunday = 0)
│ │ │ └────── Month (1 - 12)
│ │ └──────── Day of month (1 - 31)
│ └────────── Hour (0 - 23)
└──────────── Minute (0 - 59)
```

For example, this entry runs a script every day at 8 AM:

```
0 8 * * * /usr/bin/python3 /home/user/scripts/daily_report.py
```

Let's go through the steps of setting up a cron job that runs a Python script automatically.

Step 1: Create Your Python Script

Let's say you want to send a report every morning. Here's your script, saved as `daily_report.py`.

```
from datetime import datetime

def generate_report():
    now = datetime.now().strftime("%Y-%m-%d %H:%M:%S")
    with open("/home/user/reports/log.txt", "a") as file:
        file.write(f"Report generated at {now}\n")

generate_report()
```

Make sure the script is working by running it manually:

```
python3 /home/user/scripts/daily_report.py
```

Step 2: Make the Script Executable (Optional)

If you want to run it without explicitly calling Python, add a shebang at the top:

```
#!/usr/bin/env python3
```

121

Then update permissions:

```
chmod +x /home/user/scripts/daily_report.py
```

Now you can run it like this:

```
/home/user/scripts/daily_report.py
```

Step 3: Open Your Crontab

To edit the crontab for the current user:

```
crontab -e
```

If it's your first time using it, you'll be asked to choose an editor. For simplicity, select `nano`.

Step 4: Add a Cron Entry

To run the script every day at 7 AM:

```
0 7 * * * /usr/bin/python3 /home/user/scripts/daily_report.py
```

Make sure:

- You use the **absolute path** to the Python interpreter (you can find it with `which python3`)
- You also use the **full path** to your script

After saving the file and exiting, the cron job is active.

Step 5: Verify It's Working

Since cron runs in the background, it doesn't show output like the terminal does. Here are some tips to troubleshoot:

1. **Redirect output to a log file**:

```
0 7 * * * /usr/bin/python3
/home/user/scripts/daily_report.py >>
/home/user/logs/cron.log 2>&1
```

2. **Check logs**: On most systems, cron logs are available via:

```
grep CRON /var/log/syslog   # Ubuntu/Debian
tail -f /var/log/cron       # CentOS/RedHat
```

3. **Environment variables**: Cron runs with a minimal environment. You may need to define variables (like PATH) inside your script or the cron entry.

Real-World Example: Auto Cleanup Script

Here's a script that deletes files older than 7 days from a folder:

```python
import os
import time

FOLDER = "/home/user/temp/"
DAYS = 7
now = time.time()

for filename in os.listdir(FOLDER):
    path = os.path.join(FOLDER, filename)
    if os.path.isfile(path):
        if os.stat(path).st_mtime < now - DAYS * 86400:
            os.remove(path)
```

Then add to your crontab to run daily at midnight:

```
0 0 * * * /usr/bin/python3 /home/user/scripts/cleanup.py
```

When to Use Cron

Cron is ideal for:

- Scripts that need to run on a schedule regardless of system state
- Tasks that run even after logout or reboot
- Low-dependency automation that doesn't require user input

Just remember: cron doesn't "wake up" your computer—it only runs when the system is active. On laptops, ensure they're awake during the scheduled time or use a system-specific wake timer.

Wrapping Up

Cron is like a quiet personal assistant for your computer. Set it up once, and it handles the rest. Whether you're cleaning files, checking APIs, or generating reports, combining cron with Python unlocks powerful scheduling capabilities.

It's a little old-school, but incredibly reliable—which is why it's still widely used today across servers and desktops alike.

6.3 Using Windows Task Scheduler

Windows Task Scheduler is an incredibly powerful tool built into the Windows operating system. It allows you to schedule tasks (such as running scripts, applications, or system tasks) automatically at specified times or when certain conditions are met. It's Windows' answer to cron, but with a graphical interface that can make it easier for some users, especially those who prefer not to work with command-line tools.

In this guide, we'll explore how to use Windows Task Scheduler to automate your Python scripts, just like we did with cron jobs on macOS/Linux. This tool can be an absolute game-changer when you need to run tasks on a regular schedule.

Getting Started: Opening Windows Task Scheduler

To begin, you'll need to open the Task Scheduler. There are a couple of ways to do this:

1. **Via the Start Menu**:
   - Press the `Windows` key and type "Task Scheduler."
   - Click on the "Task Scheduler" application that appears.

2. **Via the Run Dialog**:
   o   Press `Win + R`, type `taskschd.msc`, and hit Enter.

Once you have Task Scheduler open, you'll see a window with the Task Scheduler Library in the left panel. This is where you can create, manage, and monitor your scheduled tasks.

Creating a New Task

Let's walk through how to create a task that runs a Python script on a schedule. Follow these steps:

1. **Create a New Task**:
   o   In the Task Scheduler window, click on the "Create Task" option in the right-hand panel.
   o   This opens a dialog box where you can define the properties of the task.
2. **General Tab**:
   o   **Name your task**: Give it a name that will help you remember what it does, like `Daily Report Script`.
   o   **Description**: You can also add a short description to remind yourself what the task does.
   o   Under "Security options," you'll have a choice of running the task only when you're logged on or whether to allow it to run whether you're logged on or not. If you select the latter, you might need to input your password when setting up the task.
3. **Triggers Tab**:
   o   Here, you can specify **when** the task should run.
   o   Click **New...** to set a new trigger. You can choose from options like:
       ▪   **Daily, Weekly, Monthly**, or **On event**.
       ▪   You can set the specific start time and frequency. For example, if you want the task to run every day at 8 AM, you'd set:
           ▪   **Begin the task**: On a schedule
           ▪   **Settings**: Daily
           ▪   **Start**: 8:00 AM
4. **Actions Tab**:
   o   Here's where you'll specify what exactly should happen when the task is triggered.

- o Click **New…** and then select **Start a Program** as the action.
- o In the **Program/script** field, type the path to the Python executable (e.g., `C:\Python39\python.exe`).
- o In the **Add arguments** field, type the path to your Python script. For example:
- o `C:\Users\YourName\Documents\python-scripts\daily_report.py`

Make sure both the Python executable and the script paths are correct. If your script relies on any additional arguments, you can add those here as well.

5. **Conditions Tab** (Optional):
   - o You can set conditions, like whether the task should only run if the computer is idle, or whether it should run only if the computer is on AC power. These options allow for more precise control over when the task runs.
6. **Settings Tab**:
   - o You can choose how the task behaves if it's already running or if it fails to start. Some useful options include:
     - **Allow the task to be run on demand**: Lets you manually trigger the task if needed.
     - **If the task fails, restart it**: This can help if you're automating something critical and want to ensure it runs without interruption.

Testing the Task

Once you've set up your task, you'll want to test it to make sure everything works smoothly.

1. **Run the Task Manually**:
   - o In the Task Scheduler window, locate your task in the **Task Scheduler Library**.
   - o Right-click on the task, and select **Run**. This will execute the task immediately.
2. **Check for Errors**:
   - o If your task doesn't run as expected, you can check the **History** tab of the task for any error messages or logs.

- o You can also check the Python script's output, especially if you've directed output to a log file (or the console).

Common Issues and Troubleshooting

- **The script doesn't run as expected**:
  - o Double-check that the path to your Python executable and script are correct.
  - o Ensure that your Python script doesn't rely on specific environment variables that may not be available to the Task Scheduler.
  - o If you have errors in your script, use logging or error handling (e.g., `try-except`) to capture them and log them to a file.
- **Permissions issues**:
  - o If you're running the task as an administrator, ensure the task is set to "Run with highest privileges" under the General tab.
  - o Some tasks require elevated privileges, and Task Scheduler might not run the script properly without the proper permissions.
- **The task doesn't run when the system is asleep**:
  - o By default, the task won't run if the system is asleep. You can change this in the Conditions tab, where you can configure the task to "Wake the computer to run this task."

Real-World Example: Sending Automated Reports

Let's say you want to send an automated report every morning at 9 AM. You would create a Python script like this:

```python
import smtplib
from email.mime.text import MIMEText
from datetime import datetime

def send_report():
    now = datetime.now().strftime("%Y-%m-%d %H:%M:%S")
    msg = MIMEText(f"Here is your report for {now}")
    msg["Subject"] = "Daily Report"
    msg["From"] = "your_email@example.com"
    msg["To"] = "recipient@example.com"
```

```
    with smtplib.SMTP("smtp.example.com", 587) as server:
        server.starttls()
        server.login("your_email@example.com",
"your_password")
        server.sendmail(msg["From"], msg["To"],
msg.as_string())

if __name__ == "__main__":
    send_report()
```

Then, in Task Scheduler, you could set it to run every day at 9 AM using the actions and triggers steps we covered earlier. The script will automatically run and send the report every morning without you having to lift a finger.

Conclusion

Windows Task Scheduler is a powerful tool for automating your Python scripts on a regular schedule. Whether you're working with simple daily tasks or more complex operations, Task Scheduler gives you the flexibility to run your Python programs exactly when you need them. It's an excellent tool for users who prefer a GUI approach over command-line tools like cron.

By following this guide, you can schedule everything from system cleanup scripts to daily reports, saving time and ensuring consistent automation. Keep exploring the full range of Task Scheduler features, and you'll find plenty of ways to boost your workflow.

6.4 Project: Daily System Cleanup Script (Sneak Peek)

Automation doesn't just save time—it can also help keep your system running smoothly by handling repetitive tasks that would otherwise take up your valuable time. In this project, we're going to develop a **Daily System Cleanup Script** using Python, which will handle tasks like clearing temporary files, deleting cache files, and ensuring your system is clean and organized every day.

By the end of this project, you'll be able to automate a variety of system maintenance tasks, keeping your computer running efficiently with minimal intervention. We'll also use Task Scheduler (on Windows) or Cron (on macOS/Linux) to schedule this cleanup task, ensuring it runs automatically every day without you having to worry about it.

Why Create a Daily System Cleanup Script?

Before we dive into the code, let's quickly review why a daily system cleanup script is useful. Over time, systems accumulate unnecessary files—temporary files, cache files, browser history, and system logs—which can consume precious disk space and slow down your computer. By automating the cleanup process, we can free up space and prevent these files from piling up.

What Will Our Script Do?

Our cleanup script will:

1. **Delete temporary files**: These are files that are created by various applications and are often left behind after an app closes.
2. **Clear browser cache and history**: Web browsers tend to store cache files to speed up your browsing experience, but these files can accumulate over time.
3. **Clean up system logs and old files**: System logs are useful for troubleshooting, but old logs can be safely removed to save space.

The end result will be a lightweight Python script that runs on a schedule and clears out unwanted files, maintaining your system's health.

Step-by-Step Guide

Let's break down the implementation of the script. We'll use a combination of Python libraries like `os`, `shutil`, and `glob` to achieve this.

1. Delete Temporary Files

Many applications generate temporary files, and these files usually reside in system-specific directories. We'll create a function that locates these files and deletes them.

129

Code Example:

```python
import os
import shutil
import tempfile

def delete_temp_files():
    temp_dir = tempfile.gettempdir()   # Gets the temp
directory for the system
    print(f"Deleting files from {temp_dir}...")

    # List all files in the temp directory
    for file in os.listdir(temp_dir):
        file_path = os.path.join(temp_dir, file)
        try:
            if os.path.isfile(file_path):
                os.remove(file_path)   # Delete the file
                print(f"Deleted {file}")
        except Exception as e:
            print(f"Error deleting {file}: {e}")
```

In this function:

- We use the `tempfile.gettempdir()` function to locate the system's temporary directory.
- We loop through all files in that directory and attempt to delete them.

This will clear out temporary files that your system doesn't need anymore.

2. Clear Browser Cache (For Chrome)

Next, we'll clear the cache files of popular browsers like Chrome. Cache files are stored in specific directories based on the browser. For Chrome, the cache files are typically stored in a specific path under your user profile.

Code Example:

```python
def clear_chrome_cache():
    cache_path = os.path.expanduser('~') +
r'\\AppData\\Local\\Google\\Chrome\\User
Data\\Default\\Cache'
    print(f"Clearing Chrome cache at {cache_path}...")

    try:
        # List all files in the cache directory and delete
them
        for file in os.listdir(cache_path):
```

130

```
        file_path = os.path.join(cache_path, file)
        if os.path.isfile(file_path):
            os.remove(file_path)
            print(f"Deleted {file}")
    except Exception as e:
        print(f"Error clearing Chrome cache: {e}")
```

Here:

- We use `os.path.expanduser('~')` to get the current user's home directory and build the path to the Chrome cache folder.
- We loop through the files in the Chrome cache folder and delete them.

You can adjust this for other browsers by modifying the cache path.

3. Clean Up System Logs

Most operating systems keep logs of system activities, and while these logs are helpful for debugging, they can quickly pile up and take up valuable disk space. We can write a function to clean up these logs. For instance, on Windows, you can delete the `Windows\Logs` directory contents, or for Linux, system logs are stored under `/var/log`.

Code Example:

```
def clean_system_logs():
    log_path = r'C:\Windows\System32\winevt\Logs'  # Path to
Windows Event Logs
    print(f"Cleaning system logs from {log_path}...")

    try:
        # Loop through all the files in the log directory and
delete them
        for file in os.listdir(log_path):
            file_path = os.path.join(log_path, file)
            if os.path.isfile(file_path):
                os.remove(file_path)
                print(f"Deleted {file}")
    except Exception as e:
        print(f"Error cleaning system logs: {e}")
```

This function:

- Locates the system logs folder and attempts to delete each file inside it.

- Logs will vary depending on the OS, so you'll need to modify the path according to your system's log folder.

Scheduling the Cleanup Script

Once the script is set up, the next step is to schedule it to run automatically. If you're using **Windows**, you can set up this task through **Windows Task Scheduler**, or if you're on **macOS/Linux**, you can use **Cron**. We've already covered how to do that in earlier chapters.

For a quick recap, we'll:

- Open Task Scheduler (or Cron on Linux).
- Set the trigger to "Daily" at a specific time (e.g., 3:00 AM).
- Set the action to run the Python script with the correct Python interpreter.

Example: Full Script

Combining everything, here's a complete version of the cleanup script that incorporates all the components we've discussed:

```python
import os
import shutil
import tempfile
import time

def delete_temp_files():
    temp_dir = tempfile.gettempdir()
    print(f"Deleting files from {temp_dir}...")

    for file in os.listdir(temp_dir):
        file_path = os.path.join(temp_dir, file)
        try:
            if os.path.isfile(file_path):
                os.remove(file_path)
                print(f"Deleted {file}")
        except Exception as e:
            print(f"Error deleting {file}: {e}")

def clear_chrome_cache():
```

```python
        cache_path = os.path.expanduser('~') +
r'\\AppData\\Local\\Google\\Chrome\\User
Data\\Default\\Cache'
    print(f"Clearing Chrome cache at {cache_path}...")

    try:
        for file in os.listdir(cache_path):
            file_path = os.path.join(cache_path, file)
            if os.path.isfile(file_path):
                os.remove(file_path)
                print(f"Deleted {file}")
    except Exception as e:
        print(f"Error clearing Chrome cache: {e}")

def clean_system_logs():
    log_path = r'C:\Windows\System32\winevt\Logs'
    print(f"Cleaning system logs from {log_path}...")

    try:
        for file in os.listdir(log_path):
            file_path = os.path.join(log_path, file)
            if os.path.isfile(file_path):
                os.remove(file_path)
                print(f"Deleted {file}")
    except Exception as e:
        print(f"Error cleaning system logs: {e}")

if __name__ == "__main__":
    print("Starting daily system cleanup...")
    delete_temp_files()
    clear_chrome_cache()
    clean_system_logs()
    print("System cleanup complete.")
```

Conclusion

With the **Daily System Cleanup Script**, you've automated an essential maintenance task that keeps your system clean, fast, and organized. By combining Python's power with scheduling tools like Task Scheduler (on Windows) or Cron (on macOS/Linux), you can ensure that this task runs seamlessly in the background.

This project is just the beginning. You can add more tasks, like clearing old downloads or defragmenting your hard drive, to tailor the script to your needs.

Chapter 7: Desktop and GUI Automation

Not all software offers an API or command-line interface. Sometimes, the only way to interact with an application is the same way a human would—by clicking, typing, and navigating menus. That's where desktop automation comes in.

In this chapter, you'll learn how to control your mouse, keyboard, and screen using Python with the `pyautogui` library. We'll start with the basics—like simulating mouse clicks and typing—then move to more advanced tasks like image recognition. Finally, you'll put it all together by building a bot that can automatically log in to a desktop application.

7.1 Controlling the Keyboard and Mouse with `pyautogui`

When you want to automate tasks that involve interacting with desktop applications—those without APIs or command-line interfaces—you need to simulate human interaction. That means controlling the mouse and keyboard just like a person would. Python's `pyautogui` library lets you do exactly that.

Let's walk through how `pyautogui` gives you full control over your screen in a way that feels almost like remote-controlling your own body—except it's your script doing the work.

Installing and Getting Started

To begin, make sure you have `pyautogui` installed:

```
pip install pyautogui
```

It works on Windows, macOS, and Linux. Once installed, import it in your Python script:

```
import pyautogui
```

At its core, `pyautogui` controls the mouse and keyboard and can even take screenshots. But to use it effectively, you need to be thoughtful—adding delays, checks, and (very importantly) a failsafe.

Mouse Control Basics

Let's look at how you can move the mouse to any part of the screen and perform clicks:

```
pyautogui.moveTo(100, 150, duration=0.5)   # Move to (x=100,
y=150) in half a second
pyautogui.click()   # Left click
```

The coordinates are based on your screen's resolution. To find out where your mouse is or how big your screen is:

```
print(pyautogui.position())      # Current mouse position
print(pyautogui.size())          # Width and height of
screen
```

You can also do more specific mouse actions:

```
pyautogui.rightClick()
pyautogui.doubleClick()
pyautogui.dragTo(300, 300, duration=1)   # Simulate dragging
```

One helpful feature is `pyautogui.displayMousePosition()`. Run it in your terminal to track your mouse coordinates in real-time—super useful when planning click locations.

Typing with the Keyboard

Typing is just as straightforward:

```
pyautogui.write('Hello, this is automated!', interval=0.1)
```

You can press individual keys too:

```
pyautogui.press('enter')
pyautogui.press(['left', 'left', 'backspace'])  # Multiple
keys
```

To send hotkeys:

```
pyautogui.hotkey('ctrl', 's')  # Simulates Ctrl+S
```

This is useful for saving files, copying data, or opening dialog boxes in GUI programs.

Using Delays and Failsafe

Here's something I learned the hard way: Always give your script time to breathe. Without delays, it's too fast to control or debug.

```
import time
time.sleep(2)  # Pause 2 seconds before starting
```

More importantly, `pyautogui` includes a built-in safety feature. If your mouse is ever in the top-left corner of your screen, it will immediately stop the script:

```
pyautogui.FAILSAFE = True
```

This should *always* be enabled during testing.

Putting It Together: Automate Notepad

Let's automate a real example. We'll open Notepad, write a message, and save the file.

```
import subprocess
import pyautogui
import time

# Step 1: Launch Notepad
subprocess.Popen('notepad.exe')
time.sleep(1)

# Step 2: Type a message
```

```
pyautogui.write("Automating with pyautogui is pretty cool!",
interval=0.1)

# Step 3: Save the file (Ctrl+S)
pyautogui.hotkey('ctrl', 's')
time.sleep(1)

# Step 4: Enter filename and hit Enter
pyautogui.write("my_automated_file.txt", interval=0.1)
pyautogui.press('enter')
```

This simple example shows how easily you can begin controlling applications. Imagine automating data entry or GUI testing with just a few more lines of code.

Final Notes

While `pyautogui` is powerful, it's important to use it responsibly. Since it controls your entire screen, accidental clicks or keystrokes can cause unintended results. Always test slowly and include a failsafe.

In real-world workflows, `pyautogui` shines when paired with image recognition or used as part of a larger automation system (you'll see this in later sections). Whether you're scheduling repetitive tasks or creating full desktop bots, mastering `pyautogui` is your first step to full GUI control.

7.2 Automating Tasks with Screenshots and Clicks

When you're working with applications that don't have APIs or scripting hooks, automating them might seem impossible. That's where screen-based automation—powered by `pyautogui`—comes in. With the ability to take screenshots and interact with specific elements on the screen, you can write scripts that visually recognize buttons, icons, or fields and interact with them like a human would.

This guide will walk you through how to use screenshots, image recognition, and precise clicking to automate virtually any desktop task.

Why Screenshots Matter in Automation

Most GUI-based applications weren't built for automation. Without APIs or script interfaces, your only option is to simulate what a person would do—move the mouse, click buttons, type, and so on. But doing that blindly (e.g., hardcoding coordinates) can break easily.

Instead of relying on static positions, `pyautogui` lets you interact with visual elements. You can take a screenshot of a button, then have your script search for that image on the screen. If it finds it, click it. If not, handle the error.

This method makes your automation scripts much more flexible and resilient.

Taking Screenshots with pyautogui

You can capture a screenshot of your entire screen or a specific region:

```
import pyautogui

screenshot = pyautogui.screenshot()
screenshot.save('full_screen.png')
```

To capture just a portion:

```
region = pyautogui.screenshot(region=(0, 0, 300, 400))  # (x,
y, width, height)
region.save('partial.png')
```

These screenshots are useful for debugging or capturing UI elements you want to search for.

Locating Images on the Screen

Once you have an image (for example, a "Save" button), you can use `locateOnScreen()` to find it:

```
location = pyautogui.locateOnScreen('save_button.png',
confidence=0.8)
```

```
if location:
    print("Button found at:", location)
else:
    print("Button not found.")
```

By default, this uses exact pixel matching. Add the `confidence` parameter (between 0 and 1) to allow for minor differences. This requires the `opencv-python` package:

```
pip install opencv-python
```

Once you find an image, you can click it:

```
pyautogui.click(location)
```

Or better, center the click:

```
center = pyautogui.center(location)
pyautogui.click(center)
```

This method ensures your click lands directly on the target.

Automating a Real Example: Click a Calculator Button

Let's simulate opening the Calculator app and clicking the number "7".

Step 1: Take a screenshot of the "7" button

Open Calculator, take a screenshot of the "7" button using your OS screenshot tool, and save it as `7_button.png` in your script folder.

Step 2: Automate the click

```
import pyautogui
import subprocess
import time

# Launch Calculator (Windows example)
subprocess.Popen('calc.exe')
time.sleep(2)

# Find the "7" button and click it
location = pyautogui.locateOnScreen('7_button.png',
confidence=0.9)
```

```
if location:
    pyautogui.click(pyautogui.center(location))
    print("Clicked the 7 button.")
else:
    print("7 button not found.")
```

You can use this same logic to click through login buttons, open files, or interact with GUI elements in legacy applications.

Automating Sequences of Visual Actions

You're not limited to one click. For example, automating a login sequence might involve:

1. Clicking on a username field.
2. Typing a username.
3. Clicking on a password field.
4. Typing a password.
5. Clicking the login button.

With image recognition, you can locate each of these elements individually.

```
def click_image(path, confidence=0.8):
    location = pyautogui.locateOnScreen(path,
confidence=confidence)
    if location:
        pyautogui.click(pyautogui.center(location))
        time.sleep(0.5)
        return True
    return False

# Click and type login credentials
if click_image('username_field.png'):
    pyautogui.write('my_username')
if click_image('password_field.png'):
    pyautogui.write('securepassword123')
click_image('login_button.png')
```

With a few reusable functions, you can create full workflows based on what your screen shows.

Tips for Reliable Automation

- **Image quality matters**: Keep screenshots clean and tightly cropped to the UI element.
- **Be resolution-aware**: If you change screen resolution or scaling, images might not match.
- **Use confidence levels wisely**: Lower confidence handles minor visual differences, but may increase false positives.
- **Slow it down**: Add `time.sleep()` between steps for better reliability, especially when apps take time to load.

Final Thoughts

Automating desktop tasks with screenshots and clicks is like giving your script a pair of eyes. It can see what's on the screen and make decisions based on that—just like a human would. This kind of automation is powerful for repetitive admin work, legacy software interactions, or even GUI testing.

It takes some patience to fine-tune, but once it's running smoothly, it can free you from hours of manual clicking.

7.3 Simple Image Recognition for GUI Tasks

In GUI automation, image recognition can be a game-changer. Instead of relying on coordinates or fixed positions, your scripts can "see" the screen, identify visual elements like buttons or icons, and interact with them—even if their location changes slightly. In this guide, we'll explore how to implement simple image recognition for GUI automation using Python and `pyautogui`, powered by OpenCV.

This technique is especially useful when you're working with software that doesn't expose any programmatic API or if elements shift position between sessions.

How Image Recognition Works in GUI Automation

The idea is simple: you provide a reference image (for example, a screenshot of a button), and your Python script scans the screen to find a match. If it sees something that closely resembles your reference image, it performs an action—like a mouse click or keyboard input.

This technique depends on *template matching*, and while it's not full-blown computer vision, it's surprisingly effective for many automation tasks.

Getting Set Up

You'll need a few libraries to get started:

```
pip install pyautogui opencv-python
```

- `pyautogui` handles the screen interactions.
- `opencv-python` allows fuzzy matching with the `confidence` parameter.

Now you're ready to begin.

Capturing a Reference Image

Start by taking a clear screenshot of the element you want your script to recognize—a button, icon, or text field. Use a tool like Snipping Tool (Windows), Screenshot (Mac), or Flameshot (Linux) and save the image in the same directory as your script. Keep the image tightly cropped for better accuracy.

Let's say you saved an image called `submit_button.png`.

Searching for the Image on Screen

Here's a simple Python script to locate and click the image on the screen:

```
import pyautogui
import time

# Pause between actions to mimic human behavior
pyautogui.PAUSE = 0.5

# Try to locate the image with a bit of tolerance
button_location =
pyautogui.locateOnScreen('submit_button.png', confidence=0.8)

if button_location:
    pyautogui.click(pyautogui.center(button_location))
    print("Button clicked!")
else:
    print("Button not found.")
```

The `confidence` parameter (0 to 1) allows flexibility in matching. This is where OpenCV helps: it enables approximate visual matches even if pixels aren't 100% identical.

You might need to adjust `confidence` depending on how clean or variable your UI is. In most cases, `0.8` is a good starting point.

Making It Reusable

Instead of duplicating matching code in every script, wrap it in a helper function:

```
def click_image(image_path, confidence=0.8):
    location = pyautogui.locateOnScreen(image_path,
confidence=confidence)
    if location:
        pyautogui.click(pyautogui.center(location))
        return True
    return False
```

This makes it easy to build higher-level automation routines.

Real-World Example: Automating a Print Dialog

Let's say you want to automate clicking the "Print" button in a desktop app.

1. Take a screenshot of the "Print" button and save it as `print_button.png`.
2. Use the function above to click it:

```
import time

print("Waiting for Print button...")
for _ in range(10):  # Try 10 times
    if click_image('print_button.png', confidence=0.9):
        print("Print initiated.")
        break
    time.sleep(1)
else:
    print("Print button not found.")
```

This script patiently waits for the button to appear and then clicks it. If the button doesn't show up within the timeout, it exits gracefully.

Common Pitfalls and How to Fix Them

- **Image not found?**
  Double-check that your screenshot matches exactly what appears on screen. Even a one-pixel border can break the match.
- **Resolution or scaling mismatch?**
  Your script and the screenshot must come from the same display setup. High DPI displays (like 4K monitors) can cause mismatches. Try running your system at 100% zoom.
- **UI animations?**
  Wait a second or two (`time.sleep(2)`) before searching for the image to allow animations to finish.
- **Use grayscale for speed** (optional):
  `locateOnScreen()` supports grayscale matching, which can be faster:

  ```
  location = pyautogui.locateOnScreen('image.png',
  confidence=0.8, grayscale=True)
  ```

When to Use (and Not Use) Image Recognition

Image-based automation is best when:

- You don't have access to code-based APIs.
- UI elements don't shift drastically between sessions.
- You're automating consistent desktop workflows.

However, it's less ideal for:

- Dynamic UIs that change frequently.
- Accessibility-focused applications (there may be better solutions like accessibility APIs).
- Situations requiring high reliability and speed.

In those cases, consider combining it with logic based on window titles, keyboard shortcuts, or even using tools like `pywinauto` or `AutoHotKey`.

Final Thoughts

Image recognition adds a powerful tool to your automation toolkit. It allows scripts to visually locate and interact with UI elements in any application, regardless of how closed-off or custom the software is. While it's not flawless, when used carefully, it can dramatically reduce repetitive manual work.

7.4 Project: Desktop App Login Bot

Automating a desktop application login process is one of the most practical and satisfying use cases for GUI automation. In this project, we'll build a **Desktop App Login Bot** using `pyautogui`. This bot will open an application (if needed), locate the login fields, enter credentials, and submit the form—all without touching your keyboard or mouse.

Whether you're logging into legacy software every day, testing desktop UIs, or automating repetitive admin tasks, this type of automation can save time and mental bandwidth.

Project Overview

The core idea is simple: your script will "see" the login screen using screenshots, move the mouse to the input fields, type the credentials, and click the login button.

This project assumes that:

- You already have the desktop app installed.
- You can manually open it and take screenshots of the username field, password field, and login button.
- The UI is consistent (pixel-perfect or close to it).

Step 1: Setup and Dependencies

Install the required package:

```
pip install pyautogui
```

Optionally, install `opencv-python` to enable fuzzy image matching:

```
pip install opencv-python
```

This allows you to use the `confidence` parameter when locating elements on the screen.

Step 2: Capture Reference Images

Manually take screenshots of:

- The **username** input field (`username_field.png`)
- The **password** input field (`password_field.png`)
- The **login** button (`login_button.png`)

Keep these images tightly cropped and store them in your project directory.

Step 3: Define Helper Functions

Start with reusable functions to click and type using image recognition:

```
import pyautogui
import time

def click_image(image_path, confidence=0.9, timeout=10):
    start_time = time.time()
    while time.time() - start_time < timeout:
        location = pyautogui.locateCenterOnScreen(image_path,
confidence=confidence)
        if location:
            pyautogui.click(location)
            return True
        time.sleep(0.5)
    raise Exception(f"Image not found: {image_path}")

def type_text(text):
    pyautogui.write(text, interval=0.05)
```

Step 4: Automate the Login

Here's the main script that brings everything together:

```
import pyautogui
import time

# Optional: Open the application first (if needed)
# import subprocess
# subprocess.Popen(['path/to/app.exe'])

time.sleep(3)  # Give time to manually switch to the login
screen

try:
    print("Clicking username field...")
    click_image('username_field.png')
    type_text('your_username')

    print("Clicking password field...")
    click_image('password_field.png')
    type_text('your_password')

    print("Clicking login button...")
    click_image('login_button.png')

    print("Login automation completed.")
```

```
except Exception as e:
    print("Error:", e)
```

You can adjust the username and password accordingly, or pull them securely from environment variables for safety:

```
import os
username = os.environ.get('LOGIN_USER')
password = os.environ.get('LOGIN_PASS')
```

Step 5: Making It Robust

GUI automation can be sensitive to screen changes, so here are a few tips:

- **Use delays** between actions. Some UIs take time to render input fields. Add short sleeps (`time.sleep(1)`) after major actions.
- **Match resolutions**. Take screenshots and run the script using the same display settings.
- **Disable animations** in your app if possible. These can interfere with image detection.

If the app changes layouts or supports themes (dark/light mode), maintain a few versions of the reference images and adapt accordingly.

Bonus: Add App Launch Logic

Want your bot to also open the app itself?

```
import subprocess

subprocess.Popen(['C:\\Program Files\\MyApp\\MyApp.exe'])
time.sleep(5)  # Adjust this depending on how long your app
takes to launch
```

Combine that with the login logic and you have a full end-to-end automation.

Use Cases and Considerations

This login bot approach works great for:

- Internal tools with no API.
- Legacy software that requires daily login.
- Automated testing of desktop login flows.

That said, it's important to **not use this for unauthorized access or in ways that violate software terms of service**. It's best used for automating your own workflows or in secure testing environments.

Final Thoughts

Automating desktop login with `pyautogui` demonstrates how effective visual automation can be. While not as precise as code-based APIs, image recognition enables you to interact with any GUI that's visually accessible. The key is accuracy and patience: the more stable your UI and environment, the more reliable your bot.

Part IV: Wrapping Up and Moving Forward

Chapter 8: Best Practices and Beyond

Automation is powerful, but like any tool, it can be tricky to use effectively without a solid understanding of the best practices. In this chapter, we'll cover crucial aspects like debugging, error handling, security, script reuse, and version control. By the end of this chapter, you'll have the knowledge to make your scripts more robust, maintainable, and ready for the real world.

8.1 Debugging and Error Handling

No matter how well you write your code, it's inevitable that errors will occur. Whether you're building an automation script, a complex web scraper, or a system utility, debugging and error handling are essential skills to master. In this section, we'll explore both of these concepts and see how you can implement them effectively to make your code more resilient and easier to maintain.

Debugging: The Process of Finding and Fixing Bugs

Debugging is the detective work of programming. It's about identifying where and why things went wrong and figuring out how to fix them. While debugging, it's easy to get frustrated, especially when you're not sure where to start. The good news is there are several techniques to help you track down issues systematically.

The most basic approach to debugging is **print statements**. This simple method involves placing `print()` calls at strategic points in your code to display the values of variables and confirm that your code is behaving as expected.

For example:

```
def add_numbers(a, b):
    print(f"Adding {a} and {b}")  # Print to track variables
    return a + b
```

```
result = add_numbers(5, 3)
print(f"Result: {result}")
```

By printing out values, you can observe how data is flowing through your program. This often gives you a clue about what might be going wrong.

More Advanced Debugging with Python's Built-in Tools

While print statements are helpful, they can clutter your code and may not always give you enough insight into the problem. For more complex bugs, Python has built-in debugging tools like the pdb module.

The Python Debugger (pdb) allows you to step through your code, inspect variables, and control execution flow interactively.

Here's an example:

```
import pdb

def divide(a, b):
    pdb.set_trace()   # Pause execution here
    return a / b

result = divide(10, 2)
print(f"Result: {result}")
```

When you run this script, Python will pause execution at the set_trace() line, allowing you to inspect variables, step through the code line by line, and evaluate expressions in real-time.

For example, when you hit the breakpoint, you can inspect variables like this:

```
(Pdb) p a
10
(Pdb) p b
2
```

You can also continue execution or step through the code line by line using commands like n (next line), c (continue), and q (quit).

If you prefer using an integrated development environment (IDE), many popular IDEs like **PyCharm**, **VSCode**, and **Eclipse** come with built-in debuggers that offer graphical interfaces to help you track down issues without manually inserting breakpoints and print statements.

Error Handling: Making Your Code Robust

While debugging is about fixing problems, **error handling** is about preventing your code from crashing when something goes wrong. It's essential to build resilience into your code, so when an unexpected situation arises, your script can handle it gracefully instead of halting abruptly.

Python's `try`, `except`, and `finally` blocks are the primary tools for error handling. Let's look at how these work:

1. **Try-Except Block**: The `try` block contains the code that might raise an error. If an error occurs, Python will jump to the `except` block, where you can define how to handle the error.

   Example:

   ```
   try:
       result = 10 / 0  # Division by zero will raise an
   error
   except ZeroDivisionError:
       print("Cannot divide by zero!")
   ```

   In this case, instead of the script crashing with an error message, it prints a custom message when division by zero occurs.

2. **Catching Multiple Exceptions**: You can handle different types of errors by specifying multiple `except` blocks. This gives you more control over how different errors are managed.

   ```
   try:
       # some code that might raise different errors
   except (ValueError, TypeError) as e:
       print(f"An error occurred: {e}")
   ```

3. **The Finally Block**: The `finally` block is executed no matter what— whether an error occurred or not. It's useful for cleanup actions, like closing files or releasing resources.

   ```
   try:
       file = open("data.txt", "r")
   ```

153

```
        # perform file operations
    except FileNotFoundError:
        print("File not found!")
    finally:
        file.close()  # Ensure the file is closed
    regardless of an error
```

Raising Custom Errors

Sometimes you want to raise an error manually based on specific conditions in your code. You can use the `raise` keyword to trigger an exception.

Example:

```
def check_positive_number(number):
    if number < 0:
        raise ValueError("The number must be positive")
    return number
```

This approach allows you to enforce rules within your code and make sure your functions receive valid inputs.

Logging: A Better Way to Trace Errors

While `print()` statements are great for debugging in a local environment, they aren't ideal for production systems. In larger projects, **logging** is a more professional way to track the flow of your program and capture errors.

Python's `logging` module allows you to record messages at different levels of importance—**DEBUG**, **INFO**, **WARNING**, **ERROR**, and **CRITICAL**. It also allows you to write logs to files for later review.

Here's how you can set up logging in Python:

```
import logging

# Configure logging
logging.basicConfig(filename='app.log', level=logging.DEBUG)

# Log a message
logging.debug("This is a debug message")
logging.error("This is an error message")
```

This will write log messages to `app.log`, which you can review later to understand what happened during script execution.

154

Key Takeaways

- **Debugging** helps you identify and fix errors during development. Use print statements, IDE debuggers, or the `pdb` module to track down issues.
- **Error handling** prevents your script from crashing unexpectedly. Use `try`, `except`, and `finally` to handle errors gracefully and ensure smooth execution.
- **Custom errors** can be raised using the `raise` keyword, allowing you to enforce rules within your code.
- **Logging** provides a more scalable and professional way to track issues in production environments.

By integrating these techniques into your scripts, you'll make your automation tasks more reliable and easier to maintain. Error handling ensures that your scripts keep running, even when things go wrong, and debugging tools help you fix issues quickly when they arise. Debugging and error handling are foundational skills that every programmer should master to write clean, professional, and dependable code.

8.2 Managing Secrets (Passwords, API Keys)

In today's world of automation, working with external services, and managing sensitive data is a common task. Whether you're integrating third-party APIs, connecting to databases, or dealing with system configurations, managing secrets—such as passwords and API keys—becomes an essential part of your workflow.

Properly handling secrets is crucial not just for the security of your project, but also for preventing accidental leaks and ensuring that sensitive information remains protected. This guide will walk you through the importance of managing secrets safely, and how you can handle them effectively in your Python projects.

Why Managing Secrets Is Critical

Every time you interact with an external service, you often need an **API key** or a **password** to authenticate your application. While it may seem harmless to hard-code these secrets directly into your code, this practice opens the door to security risks. Hardcoding sensitive information in your code makes it easy for malicious actors to access your credentials—especially when you share your code in public repositories like GitHub. This is why managing secrets in a safe and secure way is vital.

For example, imagine storing your API keys directly in your script. If you accidentally upload your code to GitHub or share it publicly, anyone who views your repository can gain access to those keys, often with devastating consequences. They could use your keys to rack up charges on paid services or even compromise your systems.

The Basics of Secrets Management

There are several best practices for handling secrets securely in your Python scripts. Let's look at some fundamental strategies for managing passwords, API keys, and other sensitive information:

1. **Never Hardcode Secrets**: Never hardcode passwords, API keys, or other secrets directly into your source code. This is the most common mistake many developers make. It's easy to just insert them as variables and move on, but this exposes you to great risks. Instead, consider using environment variables or configuration files to store your secrets.
2. **Environment Variables**: Environment variables are one of the most common and secure ways to manage secrets in Python. You can set environment variables on your system, and access them directly from your Python code using the `os` module. This approach ensures that sensitive information is never stored directly in the codebase.

   Example of setting and accessing environment variables:

   Setting the environment variable:

   On **Mac/Linux** (bash shell):

   ```
   export API_KEY="your_api_key_here"
   ```

   On **Windows**:

   ```
   set API_KEY=your_api_key_here
   ```

   Accessing the environment variable in Python:

```
import os

api_key = os.getenv("API_KEY")
print(f"Your API key is: {api_key}")
```

By using environment variables, your secrets remain out of the code and are only available in the environment at runtime.

3. **.env Files with dotenv**: A more convenient and organized method for working with environment variables, especially in development, is using a .env file. This file contains all your secrets and configuration values in a simple key-value format. You can use the python-dotenv package to load these variables into your environment automatically.

   Here's how to do it:

   o First, install python-dotenv:

   ```
   pip install python-dotenv
   ```

   o Next, create a .env file in your project directory:

   ```
   API_KEY=your_api_key_here
   DB_PASSWORD=your_password_here
   ```

   o Then, load the environment variables from this file in your Python code:

   ```
   from dotenv import load_dotenv
   import os

   load_dotenv()  # Load environment variables from
   .env file

   api_key = os.getenv("API_KEY")
   print(f"Your API key is: {api_key}")
   ```

This method allows you to keep your credentials separate from your code and still load them dynamically, making it easier to switch between environments (e.g., development, staging, production) without exposing your secrets.

4. **Secrets Management Services**: For more advanced projects, especially in production, consider using a dedicated secrets management service. These services offer robust features, such as encryption, fine-grained access control, and auditing.

   Some popular services include:

   o **AWS Secrets Manager**: A fully managed service that enables you to store and retrieve secrets.
   o **Azure Key Vault**: A cloud service that allows you to securely store keys, passwords, and other sensitive data.
   o **HashiCorp Vault**: A tool for managing secrets and protecting sensitive data in modern infrastructure.

   These services handle the encryption and security of your secrets, while providing you with an easy way to manage access across different environments.

5. **Configuration Files**: In some cases, you may want to store your secrets in a configuration file, such as a JSON or YAML file. However, be cautious with this method, as these files should not be exposed or committed to version control (e.g., Git). If you use this approach, ensure you include the config files in .gitignore or equivalent to keep them from being tracked by version control systems.

   Example of a JSON config file (config.json):

   ```
   {
       "API_KEY": "your_api_key_here",
       "DB_PASSWORD": "your_password_here"
   }
   ```

   Reading the config file in Python:

   ```
   import json

   with open("config.json") as f:
       config = json.load(f)

   api_key = config["API_KEY"]
   print(f"Your API key is: {api_key}")
   ```

6. **Encryption**: If you absolutely must store secrets in a file (e.g., a database password for local development), consider encrypting them. Python provides libraries like `cryptography` that can help you encrypt and decrypt sensitive information when necessary.

Example of encrypting and decrypting data using the `cryptography` library:

```
pip install cryptography
from cryptography.fernet import Fernet

# Generate a key and encrypt the data
key = Fernet.generate_key()
cipher = Fernet(key)
encrypted_data = cipher.encrypt(b"my_secret_data")

# Decrypt the data
decrypted_data = cipher.decrypt(encrypted_data)
print(decrypted_data.decode())  # Output:
my_secret_data
```

This ensures that even if someone gains access to your files, the sensitive information will be protected by encryption.

Key Takeaways

- **Never hardcode secrets** directly into your codebase. Use environment variables or dedicated secrets management systems instead.
- **Environment variables** are a simple yet powerful way to manage secrets locally.
- Use a **.env file** in combination with the `python-dotenv` package for better organization of environment variables during development.
- For production systems, leverage **secrets management services** like AWS Secrets Manager or HashiCorp Vault to securely store and access sensitive data.
- Ensure that sensitive data is **encrypted** if you must store it in files or databases.
- Always be cautious when working with secrets and follow best practices to prevent accidental exposure.

By following these best practices for managing secrets, you can ensure that your Python projects remain secure, even as you automate complex tasks and integrate with external services.

8.3 Structuring Scripts for Reuse

When you're building automation scripts, whether for personal projects or professional applications, it's essential to structure your code in a way that allows for reuse and scalability. The last thing you want is to find yourself writing the same code repeatedly or dealing with a tangled, hard-to-maintain script. Reusable code isn't just about efficiency—it's about writing clean, modular, and maintainable programs that can adapt to changes over time.

In this section, we'll walk through the key principles of structuring your Python scripts for reuse, emphasizing the benefits of modularity, readability, and flexibility. The goal is to create code that can easily be adapted to different tasks, extended for future requirements, and tested effectively.

The Importance of Code Structure

Before diving into specifics, it's helpful to understand why the structure of your scripts matters. A well-organized script makes it easier to:

- **Maintain**: When you need to update, debug, or improve your script, having a clear structure means you'll spend less time tracking down issues.
- **Extend**: Reusable code is designed to handle future needs, whether that means adding new functionality or integrating with other tools.
- **Collaborate**: If others need to work with your code, having a structured and organized script makes it easier for them to understand and contribute.

The way you structure your script affects its future usability. Let's take a look at how to make your Python code modular, readable, and easily adaptable.

1. Modular Design: Breaking Code into Functions and Classes

The first step in creating reusable code is to break your script into small, manageable components. In Python, these components often take the form of **functions** and **classes**.

- **Functions**: A function should perform a single task. Whether it's downloading a file, processing data, or sending an email, each function should have a clear purpose. By encapsulating specific tasks in functions, you make your code reusable, as you can call these functions from anywhere within the script—or even from other scripts.

  For example, if you're automating the process of sending an email, you could create a reusable function:

  ```python
  import smtplib
  from email.mime.text import MIMEText

  def send_email(recipient, subject, body):
      sender = "your_email@example.com"
      password = "your_password"

      msg = MIMEText(body)
      msg["Subject"] = subject
      msg["From"] = sender
      msg["To"] = recipient

      with smtplib.SMTP("smtp.example.com") as server:
          server.login(sender, password)
          server.sendmail(sender, recipient, msg.as_string())
  ```

  Here, `send_email()` encapsulates the logic needed to send an email. Whenever you need to send an email, you can call this function, passing in the recipient, subject, and body.

- **Classes**: When your code becomes more complex, you may want to organize related functions into classes. A class groups related methods (functions) and variables (data) together, which makes your code more structured. This is especially useful when you have objects that need to maintain state across multiple function calls.

161

For instance, you could create a class for automating tasks related to sending an email:

```
class EmailSender:
    def __init__(self, sender_email, password):
        self.sender_email = sender_email
        self.password = password

    def send_email(self, recipient, subject, body):
        msg = MIMEText(body)
        msg["Subject"] = subject
        msg["From"] = self.sender_email
        msg["To"] = recipient

        with smtplib.SMTP("smtp.example.com") as server:
            server.login(self.sender_email, self.password)
            server.sendmail(self.sender_email, recipient, msg.as_string())
```

Here, the `EmailSender` class keeps track of the sender's email and password and provides a method to send an email. This class can now be easily reused by creating instances for different senders, maintaining flexibility.

2. Using Configurations for Reusability

Another important aspect of structuring for reuse is separating the configuration data from your code. For example, rather than hardcoding API keys or file paths into your script, it's best practice to load this information from a separate configuration file or environment variables.

You can store configuration in a simple `.json` or `.yaml` file, or use environment variables. Here's an example of a `config.json`:

```
{
  "api_key": "your_api_key_here",
  "email_sender": "your_email@example.com",
  "smtp_server": "smtp.example.com"
}
```

In your Python code, you would load the configuration data like this:

```
import json
```

```
def load_config(file="config.json"):
    with open(file) as f:
        return json.load(f)

config = load_config()
api_key = config["api_key"]
email_sender = config["email_sender"]
```

By separating configuration data, you make the code more flexible—just modify the configuration file instead of rewriting the script.

3. Reusing Code with Libraries and Modules

When your scripts grow larger, it's worth organizing them into multiple files (modules) and directories. Python allows you to split your code into multiple files, each of which can handle a specific responsibility. This modularity helps you keep your code clean, organized, and easily reusable.

For example, you could have:

- `email_sender.py` for email-related functions and classes
- `file_handler.py` for file operations like reading and writing data
- `main.py` for orchestrating everything and running the main logic

Each module can be imported into others. For instance, in `main.py`, you could import the email functionality like this:

```
from email_sender import EmailSender

email_sender = EmailSender("your_email@example.com",
"your_password")
email_sender.send_email("recipient@example.com", "Subject",
"Email body")
```

This organization allows you to keep each file focused on a specific set of tasks, making it easier to find and modify specific functionality. It also enables you to reuse the modules across different projects.

4. Keeping Your Code DRY (Don't Repeat Yourself)

A key principle of reusable code is ensuring that you don't repeat yourself. The DRY principle encourages you to avoid writing the same logic multiple times. This leads to cleaner, more maintainable code.

For example, if you need to parse a date in several places in your script, instead of writing the date parsing logic each time, you can create a function or a method to handle it:

```
from datetime import datetime

def parse_date(date_string):
    return datetime.strptime(date_string, "%Y-%m-%d")

# Now use parse_date() wherever needed
date = parse_date("2021-08-10")
```

By isolating repetitive logic into functions, you reduce errors and make it easier to maintain and extend your code in the future.

5. Testing and Documenting Reusable Code

For your reusable code to be reliable, you should **test** it and **document** how it should be used. This will help you—and others—understand the purpose of each function and ensure that it behaves correctly.

- **Testing**: Writing tests for your functions and classes ensures that they behave as expected. The **unittest** or **pytest** modules in Python can help you write and run tests.

  Example of a simple unit test for the `send_email` function:

  ```
  import unittest

  class TestEmailSender(unittest.TestCase):
      def test_send_email(self):
          email_sender =
  EmailSender("test_email@example.com", "password")

          self.assertTrue(email_sender.send_email("recipient@example.com", "Subject", "Body"))

  if __name__ == "__main__":
      unittest.main()
  ```

- **Documentation**: Good documentation is essential for reusable code. Include docstrings in your functions and classes, explaining what they do, what parameters they accept, and what they return.

  Example of a function with a docstring:

```python
def send_email(recipient, subject, body):
    """
    Sends an email with the given subject and body to
    the recipient.

    Parameters:
        recipient (str): The email address of the
    recipient.
        subject (str): The subject of the email.
        body (str): The body content of the email.

    Returns:
        bool: True if the email was sent successfully,
    False otherwise.
    """
    # Email sending logic here
```

Conclusion

Structuring your Python scripts for reuse is all about organizing your code in a way that makes it easy to maintain, extend, and share. Whether it's by using functions, classes, configuration files, or modules, reusable code is cleaner, easier to debug, and adaptable to future needs. By adhering to these principles, you'll make your automation projects more scalable and efficient, while saving time in the long run.

8.4 Introduction to Version Control with Git

Version control is one of the most important tools in modern software development. It allows developers to track changes, collaborate with others, and maintain a history of their codebase. While there are several version control systems available, **Git** has become the industry standard due to its speed, flexibility, and ease of use. Whether you're working solo on a personal project or collaborating with a team, version control ensures that your code remains organized, manageable, and easy to maintain.

In this guide, we'll introduce you to Git and version control, and walk through the fundamental concepts and commands that will help you get started with using Git for your automation projects. By the end, you'll understand how to set up Git in your workflow, track changes, and collaborate effectively.

What is Git?

At its core, **Git** is a distributed version control system (VCS). Unlike centralized version control systems, where all files are stored in a central repository, Git keeps a complete history of your project on your local machine. This means that you can work offline, make changes, and only sync with the central repository when you're ready. Git also allows multiple versions of a project to exist simultaneously, making it easy to branch out and experiment without affecting the main codebase.

Why Should You Use Git?

The primary benefits of using Git include:

- **Tracking Changes**: You can track the history of every modification to your code, including who made the change and why. This makes debugging easier, as you can revert to a previous state of your project if something goes wrong.
- **Collaboration**: Git makes it easy for multiple people to work on the same project without overwriting each other's work. By using branches and merging them back together, Git helps maintain a smooth workflow even with a large team.
- **Backup**: Git allows you to push your changes to remote repositories like GitHub, GitLab, or Bitbucket. This serves as a backup and makes your project available across different machines.

Setting Up Git

Before you can start using Git, you'll need to install it. Git is available for **Windows**, **MacOS**, and **Linux**. If you don't have Git installed, you can download it from git-scm.com.

After installation, you'll need to configure your Git username and email. Open a terminal (or Git Bash on Windows) and run these commands:

```
git config --global user.name "Your Name"
git config --global user.email "your_email@example.com"
```

This information will be associated with every commit you make.

166

Starting a Git Repository

Once Git is set up, you can initialize a new Git repository in any directory on your computer. Navigate to your project folder and run the following command:

```
git init
```

This creates a hidden `.git` directory in your project folder, which Git will use to track changes.

Adding Files to Git

Once you've initialized the repository, you'll want to add the files you want to track. You can add a single file using:

```
git add filename.py
```

Or add all files in the directory:

```
git add .
```

This command stages the files for committing, which means Git is now tracking changes to those files. The next step is to commit those changes to the repository.

Committing Changes

A commit is a snapshot of your project at a specific point in time. After you've staged your changes with `git add`, you can commit them with:

```
git commit -m "Your commit message"
```

The commit message should briefly describe what changes were made. Good commit messages make it easy to understand the history of a project. For example, instead of just saying "fix bug," you might say "Fix issue with email sender not handling timeouts."

Viewing History

One of Git's powerful features is its ability to track the history of changes. To view the commit history, you can run:

```
git log
```

This will show a list of all the commits, including the commit ID, the author, the date, and the commit message. You can scroll through the history to see how the project has evolved over time.

Working with Branches

Branches allow you to work on different versions of your project simultaneously. You can create a branch to experiment with new features without affecting the main codebase. To create a new branch, use:

```
git branch new-feature
```

To switch to that branch:

```
git checkout new-feature
```

Now, you can make changes to the code in this branch. When you're satisfied with your changes, you can merge them back into the main branch (usually called `master` or `main`):

```
git checkout main
git merge new-feature
```

This merges the changes from the `new-feature` branch into the `main` branch.

Remote Repositories: Pushing and Pulling Changes

While Git allows you to manage your project locally, you'll often want to back up your code or collaborate with others using remote repositories (e.g., GitHub, GitLab, Bitbucket). To connect your local Git repository to a remote repository, you first need to add the remote repository URL:

```
git remote add origin https://github.com/yourusername/your-repository.git
```

To push your local commits to the remote repository, use:

```
git push origin main
```

This uploads your commits to the remote repository. If someone else has made changes to the repository, you can pull those changes into your local copy with:

```
git pull origin main
```

Cloning a Repository

If you want to contribute to an existing project or start from a remote repository, you can clone it to your local machine. This creates a copy of the repository and its entire history:

```
git clone https://github.com/yourusername/your-repository.git
```

Handling Merge Conflicts

When working with branches and merging, you might encounter **merge conflicts**. This happens when two branches have made changes to the same line of code or file. Git can't automatically decide which change should take priority, so it marks the conflict and requires manual intervention.

In the case of a merge conflict, Git will mark the conflicting sections in the file, and you'll need to resolve the conflict by choosing which version of the code to keep. After resolving the conflict, stage and commit the changes as usual:

```
git add conflicted_file.py
git commit -m "Resolve merge conflict in conflicted_file.py"
```

Conclusion

Git is an essential tool for anyone working on projects, large or small. It not only helps track the history of your work but also enables collaboration, version control, and easy code management. By understanding how to initialize repositories, commit changes, use branches, and interact with remote repositories, you'll be able to manage your automation projects with confidence.

8.5 Next Steps in Your Automation Journey

Congratulations! You've now completed a significant part of your journey in learning automation with Python. By building automation scripts, exploring libraries like `smtplib`, `pyautogui`, and `schedule`, and tackling real-world projects, you've already gained valuable skills that will serve you well in a variety of scenarios. However, as with any new skill, the journey doesn't end here. There are always more tools to explore, more techniques to master, and more complex problems to solve.

In this section, we'll look at what comes next in your automation journey. We'll discuss how you can expand your skills, deepen your knowledge, and start applying automation to more sophisticated and impactful use cases.

1. Refining and Expanding Your Skills

Automation is a broad field, and while you've gained a solid foundation, there's always room to improve. Here are some key areas you might consider diving deeper into:

- **Advanced Libraries and Frameworks**: As you continue to automate, you'll come across libraries that enable more powerful automation workflows. For instance, **Selenium** for web browser automation, **Pandas** for data manipulation, or **Flask/Django** for web-based applications. Each of these libraries opens up new opportunities for creating robust automation scripts.
- **Error Handling and Debugging**: While you've learned some basic debugging techniques, error handling is a critical skill to master. The more complex your automation scripts become, the more likely you'll run into unexpected issues. Learning how to handle and recover from errors will help you build more reliable automation systems.
- **Parallel Processing and Async Programming**: For more efficient and scalable automation tasks, learning how to execute multiple tasks simultaneously can be a game-changer. This is particularly useful for tasks that are slow or need to handle many items, like web scraping or large-scale file management. The **asyncio** library or multi-threading in Python are powerful tools to explore.
- **Advanced GUI Automation**: While you've already dipped into controlling the mouse and keyboard with `pyautogui`, you can go deeper into more complex GUI automation tasks, like automating

interactions with specific apps, developing desktop bots, or using machine learning for more intelligent automation.

2. Building More Complex Projects

With the skills you've gained, you're ready to take on more challenging projects. Automating real-world tasks is a great way to not only practice your skills but also make a meaningful impact. Consider some of the following:

- **Business Process Automation (BPA)**: Automating routine business tasks, such as report generation, database updates, or monitoring systems, can save you or your team a significant amount of time. You can start automating your day-to-day tasks at work or in personal projects and scale them into full business workflows.
- **Automation for Data Science**: Data analysis, data extraction, and reporting are tasks that can be easily automated. Integrating automation with tools like **Pandas** or **Jupyter Notebooks** can streamline the process of collecting, cleaning, analyzing, and visualizing data. You can even create automatic data pipelines for real-time data processing.
- **Home Automation**: If you're into smart homes, there's a lot of room to automate tasks like controlling lights, security cameras, and other IoT devices. Tools like **Home Assistant** or integrating with APIs from smart devices can be a fun way to apply your skills in a practical, day-to-day environment.
- **Building Bots**: The world of bot-building extends beyond simple desktop apps and can encompass bots for social media, messaging platforms (like Discord, Telegram, or Slack), or even bots for games. Developing bots that perform tasks for you, whether it's posting content, managing conversations, or automating processes in online communities, can be both rewarding and challenging.

3. Learning from the Community and Contributing

The world of automation is vast, and you can't learn it all by yourself. Fortunately, there are plenty of resources and communities to help you grow. Here are some ways you can continue your journey:

- **Contribute to Open Source Projects**: Once you're comfortable with your skills, contributing to open source projects can be a great way to learn from others and give back to the community. Open source projects often have issues that need solving, and by tackling these, you can refine your skills and connect with other automation enthusiasts.

- **Engage with the Python and Automation Communities**: Join online forums like Stack Overflow, Reddit's r/learnpython, or specialized forums in the automation space. By asking questions, sharing your projects, and learning from others, you'll expand your knowledge and grow as a programmer.
- **Learn from Others' Projects**: Github is a treasure trove of real-world projects. By exploring repositories, you can learn how others are solving similar problems and get inspiration for your own projects.
- **Online Courses and Tutorials**: There are always new frameworks, tools, and methodologies in the world of programming. Websites like Coursera, Udemy, and freeCodeCamp offer in-depth courses that can take your skills to the next level. These resources often provide a structured learning path that can help you tackle more advanced topics.

4. Exploring Automation Beyond Python

While Python is an excellent language for automation, you may eventually encounter situations where other tools or languages are better suited for certain tasks. Some areas to explore include:

- **Automation with Bash/Shell Scripts**: On Linux and macOS, shell scripting is a powerful way to automate system-level tasks. For example, automating backups, managing files, or handling system processes.
- **DevOps and CI/CD Pipelines**: Automation is central to DevOps practices. Tools like **Docker**, **Kubernetes**, and CI/CD services such as **Jenkins** can help automate deployment pipelines and infrastructure management.
- **Cloud Automation**: With the rise of cloud services, automating tasks across cloud platforms like AWS, Azure, or Google Cloud is becoming increasingly important. You can use services like **AWS Lambda** or **Azure Functions** to automate serverless tasks in the cloud.

5. Stay Curious and Keep Experimenting

One of the key aspects of learning programming is maintaining curiosity. As you continue building automation projects, you'll encounter new problems that will require new solutions. Keep experimenting with different tools, techniques, and frameworks. Try building something that challenges you and forces you to learn something new. Whether it's a new API, a different library, or a complex system, the more you explore, the more you'll grow as an automation expert.

Conclusion

Automation is an ongoing journey that continually evolves as new tools and techniques emerge. Now that you've completed this chapter, you have a strong foundation in automation with Python and are well on your way to creating complex and powerful automated systems.

Don't be afraid to take on bigger challenges and push your skills further. Whether you're building larger projects, learning from the community, or exploring new languages and technologies, the path to mastering automation is both exciting and rewarding. Keep coding, keep automating, and keep growing. Your journey has just begun!

Appendices

As you've explored the core topics in this book, there are a few supplementary resources that can make your journey even more efficient and enjoyable. These appendices will help you find quick references for Python syntax, introduce you to more Python automation libraries, provide some useful tools and resources, and spark your creativity with project ideas. Think of these as your go-to resources whenever you need a refresher or inspiration to push your automation skills to the next level.

A. Quick Python Syntax Reference

Whether you're a beginner or an experienced programmer, sometimes you just need a quick refresher on Python syntax. This reference will cover some of the most common and essential syntax structures, along with examples to get you back on track quickly.

1. **Variables and Data Types**
    - Variables in Python don't need explicit declaration. You can simply assign a value:

    ```
    x = 10   # integer
    name = "Alice"  # string
    price = 19.99  # float
    is_active = True   # boolean
    ```

2. **Basic Data Structures**
    - **Lists**: Ordered collection, can be changed.

    ```
    fruits = ["apple", "banana", "cherry"]
    ```

    - **Tuples**: Immutable collection.

    ```
    point = (3, 4)
    ```

    - **Dictionaries**: Key-value pairs.

    ```
    user = {"name": "Alice", "age": 25}
    ```

174

- **Sets**: Unordered collection of unique elements.

```
colors = {"red", "blue", "green"}
```

3. **Control Flow**
   - **If-Else Statement**:

```
if x > 10:
    print("Greater than 10")
else:
    print("Not greater than 10")
```

   - **Loops**:
     - **For Loop**: Iterate over a sequence.

```
for fruit in fruits:
    print(fruit)
```

     - **While Loop**: Repeat until a condition is met.

```
i = 0
while i < 5:
    print(i)
    i += 1
```

4. **Functions**
   - Defining a function:

```
def greet(name):
    return f"Hello, {name}!"
print(greet("Alice"))
```

5. **Error Handling**
   - Using `try` and `except` blocks:

```
try:
    result = 10 / 0
except ZeroDivisionError:
    print("Cannot divide by zero")
```

6. **List Comprehensions**
   - Efficient way to create lists:

```
squares = [x**2 for x in range(10)]
print(squares)
```

175

B. Common Python Automation Libraries

Python has a rich ecosystem of libraries that make automation tasks more manageable. Below are some of the most commonly used libraries for automation.

1. **Requests**
   - **Purpose**: Web scraping, APIs, HTTP requests.
   - **Key Functionality**: Sending HTTP requests and handling responses.

   ```
   import requests
   response = requests.get('https://example.com')
   print(response.text)
   ```

2. **BeautifulSoup**
   - **Purpose**: Web scraping and parsing HTML/XML documents.
   - **Key Functionality**: Extracting data from web pages.

   ```
   from bs4 import BeautifulSoup
   soup = BeautifulSoup(response.text,
   'html.parser')
   print(soup.find('h1').text)
   ```

3. **Selenium**
   - **Purpose**: Automating web browsers.
   - **Key Functionality**: Interacting with web pages, clicking buttons, submitting forms.

   ```
   from selenium import webdriver
   driver = webdriver.Chrome()
   driver.get('https://example.com')
   driver.find_element_by_name('q').send_keys('Pytho
   n automation')
   driver.quit()
   ```

4. **pyautogui**
   - **Purpose**: Automating mouse and keyboard actions.
   - **Key Functionality**: Clicking, typing, and taking screenshots.

   ```
   import pyautogui
   pyautogui.click(100, 200)
   pyautogui.write("Hello, World!")
   ```

5. **Pandas**
   - o **Purpose**: Data manipulation and analysis.
   - o **Key Functionality**: Handling large datasets, data cleaning, and manipulation.

```python
import pandas as pd
df = pd.read_csv('data.csv')
df.head()
```

6. **schedule**
   - o **Purpose**: Task scheduling and automation.
   - o **Key Functionality**: Running Python functions at specific times.

```python
import schedule
import time

def job():
    print("Task is running!")

schedule.every(10).seconds.do(job)
while True:
    schedule.run_pending()
    time.sleep(1)
```

7. **pyttsx3**
   - o **Purpose**: Text-to-speech conversion.
   - o **Key Functionality**: Converting written text to spoken words.

```python
import pyttsx3
engine = pyttsx3.init()
engine.say("Hello, this is an automated voice")
engine.runAndWait()
```

C. Useful Tools and Resources

Here are a few tools and online resources that can help you on your automation journey.

1. **Online Python Compiler**: Websites like Repl.it and Google Colab allow you to write and execute Python code directly in your browser without the need for local setup.

2. **GitHub**: The largest platform for hosting and sharing code. You can explore automation projects, contribute to open-source repositories, or start your own project.
3. **Stack Overflow**: A community-driven Q&A site where you can find solutions to coding problems or ask questions if you're stuck.
4. **PyPI (Python Package Index)**: This is where you can find almost any Python package or library to extend the capabilities of your automation scripts. Visit https://pypi.org/ for more details.
5. **Documentation**: Never underestimate the power of official documentation. Each library mentioned has a comprehensive and detailed guide. When in doubt, refer to the Python documentation and the respective library's docs.

D. Automation Project Ideas

Looking for inspiration? Here are some automation project ideas to fuel your creativity and practice your skills:

1. **Automated Report Generation**: Set up a script to automatically generate daily, weekly, or monthly reports from CSV or database files, and email them to relevant stakeholders.
2. **File Backup and Organization**: Automate the process of backing up important files and organizing them into directories based on file type or modification date.
3. **Social Media Automation**: Build a bot that automatically posts to your social media accounts, interacts with your followers, or scrapes data from social media for analysis.
4. **Web Scraping Bot**: Create a bot that extracts product information (like price, description, and availability) from an e-commerce website and sends updates when there are price drops or stock changes.
5. **Task Reminder Bot**: Build a bot that integrates with email, Slack, or Telegram to remind you of tasks, deadlines, or appointments.
6. **Personal Finance Tracker**: Automate your personal finance tracking by parsing bank statements or transaction data and creating monthly expense reports.
7. **Automated Testing Suite**: If you're familiar with web development, you could use Selenium to build automated testing for your web apps, ensuring they're working as expected.

Final Thoughts

With this comprehensive set of appendices, you now have a valuable set of tools and references to guide you as you continue your journey into automation. Whether you're looking to refresh your knowledge of Python syntax, discover new libraries to use in your projects, or get inspiration for your next big automation challenge, these appendices will be there to support you.

Keep exploring, keep experimenting, and most importantly, keep automating! The possibilities are endless, and with the knowledge you've gained, you're well-equipped to tackle whatever challenges lie ahead. Happy automating!

www.ingramcontent.com/pod-product-compliance
Lightning Source LLC
LaVergne TN
LVHW080116070326
832902LV00015B/2623